Busy Ant Maths

Stretch and Challenge 2

A problem-solving, cross-curricular programme for children working above end-of-year expectations

Peter Clarke

Published by Collins

An imprint of HarperCollinsPublishers
The News Building
1 London Bridge Street
London SE1 9GF

Browse the complete Collins catalogue at
www.collins.co.uk

© HarperCollins*Publishers* Limited 2016

10 9 8 7 6 5 4 3 2

ISBN 978-0-00-816731-8

British Library Cataloguing in Publication Data
A Catalogue record for this publication is available from the British Library.

Commissioned by Fiona McGlade
Cover and series design by Kneath Associates
Template creation by Ken Vail Graphic Design
Illustrations by Mark Walker, Steve Evans, Gwyneth Williamson and QBS Learning
Typesetting by QBS Learning
Editing and proofreading by Alissa McWhinnie

Printed and bound by Printed by CPI Group (UK) Ltd, Croydon, CR0 4YY

Acknowledgements
Peter Clarke wishes to thank Brian Molyneaux for his valuable contribution to this publication.

Contents

Domain(s)	Topic	Issue number	Teacher's notes page number
Number: – Number and place value	Number	1	96
	Number	2	99
	Number	3	102
	Number	4	105
Number: – Addition and subtraction	Addition	5	108
	Addition	6	111
	Subtraction	7	114
	Subtraction	8	117
Number: – Multiplication and division	Multiplication	9	120
	Multiplication	10	124
	Division	11	128
	Division	12	132
Number: – Addition and subtraction – Multiplication and division	Mixed operations	13	135
	Mixed operations	14	139
	Mixed operations	15	143
	Mixed operations	16	147
	Mixed operations	17	151
Number: – Fractions	Fractions	18	154
	Fractions	19	158
	Fractions	20	162
Measurement	Length and height	21	165
	Mass	22	168
	Capacity and volume	23	171
	Time	24	174
	Measurement	25	178
	Measurement	26	181
Geometry: – Properties of shapes	2-D shapes	27	184
	3-D shapes	28	187
	Symmetry	29	190
Geometry: – Position and direction	Position and direction	30	194
	Movement and angle	31	197
Geometry: – Properties of shapes – Position and direction	Geometry	32	200
	Geometry	33	203
Statistics	Statistics	34	206
	Statistics	35	209
	Statistics	36	212

Introduction

The National Curriculum emphasises the importance of all children mastering the programme of study taught each year and discourages the acceleration of children into content from subsequent years.

The National Curriculum states: *'The expectation is that the majority of pupils will move through the programmes of study at broadly the same pace. However, decisions about when to progress should always be based on the security of pupils' understanding and their readiness to progress to the next stage. Pupils who grasp concepts rapidly should be challenged through being offered rich and sophisticated problems before any acceleration through new content. Those who are not sufficiently fluent with earlier material should consolidate their understanding, including through additional practice, before moving on.'* [1]

However, the National Curriculum also goes on to say that: *'Within each key stage, schools [therefore] have the flexibility to introduce content earlier or later than set out in the programme of study. In addition, schools can introduce key stage content during an earlier key stage, if appropriate.'* [2]

Stretch and Challenge aims to provide support in meeting the needs of those children who are exceeding age-related expectations by providing a range of problem-solving and cross-curricular activities designed to enrich and deepen children's mathematical knowledge, skills and understanding.

The series provides opportunities for children to reason mathematically and to solve increasingly complex problems, doing so with fluency, as described in the aims of the National Curriculum:

'The National Curriculum for mathematics aims to ensure that all pupils:

- *become* **fluent** *in the fundamentals of mathematics, including through varied and frequent practice with increasingly complex problems over time, so that pupils develop conceptual understanding and the ability to recall and apply knowledge rapidly and accurately*

- **reason mathematically** *by following a line of enquiry, conjecturing relationships and generalisations, and developing an argument, justification or proof using mathematical language*

- *can* **solve problems** *by applying their mathematics to a variety of routine and non-routine problems with increasing sophistication, including breaking down problems into a series of simpler steps and persevering in seeking solutions.'* [3]

Stretch and Challenge has been designed to provide:

- a flexible 'dip-in' resource that can easily be adapted to meet the needs of individual children, and different classroom and school organisational arrangements

- enrichment activities that require children to use and apply their mathematical knowledge, skills and understanding to reason mathematically and to solve increasingly complex problems

- mathematical activities linked to the entire primary curriculum, thereby ensuring a range of cross-curricular contexts

- an easy-to-use bank of activities to save teachers time in thinking up new enrichment activities

- an interesting, unique and consistent approach to presenting enrichment activities to children.

The *Stretch and Challenge* series consists of six packs, also available digitally on Collins Connect, one for each year group from Year 1 to Year 6.

---

1 Mathematics programmes of study: key stages 1 and 2 National Curriculum in England, September 2013, page 3

2 Mathematics programmes of study: key stages 1 and 2 National Curriculum in England, September 2013, page 4

3 Mathematics programmes of study: key stages 1 and 2 National Curriculum in England, September 2013, page 3

Printed resources

Containing:

- Pupil activity booklets (Issues)
- Teacher's notes
- Resource sheets

Online resources at connect.collins.co.uk

Containing editable:

- Pupil activity booklets (Issues)
- Teacher's notes
- Resource sheets

It is envisaged that the activities in *Stretch and Challenge* will be used by either individuals or pairs of children. However, given the flexible nature of the resource, if appropriate, children can work in groups. The activities are intended to be used:

- as additional work to be done once children have finished other set work
- by those children who grasp concepts rapidly and need to be challenged through rich and sophisticated problems
- as in-depth work that is to be undertaken over a prolonged period of time, such as during the course of several lessons, a week or a particular unit of work
- as a resource for promoting mathematical reasoning and problem solving and developing independent thinking and learning
- as a springboard for further investigations into mathematics based on the children's suggestions.

The features of *Stretch and Challenge*

Pupil activity booklets (Issues)

- Each of the 36 Issues in *Stretch and Challenge 2* consists of a four-page A5 pupil activity booklet (to be printed double sided onto one sheet of A4 paper).

- The 36 Issues cover the different domains and attainment targets of the Mathematics National Curriculum Programme of Study (see pages 11–17).

- The Issues have been designed to resemble a newspaper, with each of the Issues consisting of between five and eight different activities, all related to the same mathematical topic.

- It is important to note that children are not expected to complete all the activities in an Issue nor work their way through an Issue from beginning to end. For many children not all of the activities offered in an Issue will be appropriate. When choosing which activities a child is to complete, teachers should ensure that the activities do not accelerate the child into mathematical content they may not be familiar with, or are unable to reason more deeply in order to develop a conceptual understanding. Rather, activities should be chosen on the basis that they engage the child in reasoning and the development of mathematical thinking, as well as enriching and deepening the child's mathematical knowledge, skills and understanding.

- The terms 'Issue' and 'Volume' have been used rather than 'Unit' and 'Year group' because they are in keeping with the newspaper theme.

Types of activities

- Each of the 36 Issues in *Stretch and Challenge 2* are designed to deepen children's mathematical knowledge, skills and understanding, and enhance their use and application of mathematics. There are four different types of 'using and applying' activities in the series:

   What's the Problem?   The Puzzler

   Looking for Patterns   Let's Investigate

- Alongside developing children's problem-solving skills, the series also provides activities with cross-curricular links to other subjects in the primary curriculum. The following shows the *Stretch and Challenge* features and its corresponding primary curriculum subject.

Curriculum subject	Stretch and Challenge feature
English	The Language of Maths
Science	Focus on Science
Computing	Technology Today
Geography	Around the World
History	In the Past
Art and design / Music	The Arts Roundup
Design and Technology	Construct
Physical Education	Sports Update

- As well as the features mentioned above, other regular features in *Stretch and Challenge* include:

   Money Matters   At Home (home–school link activities).

- A chart showing the link between the Issues, the *Stretch and Challenge* features and cross-curricular links can be found on pages 18 and 19.

- Inquisitive ant is a recurring feature of the series. In each Issue there is an ant holding a mathematical word or symbol. Children locate the ant and write about the meaning of the word or symbol.

Introduction

Teacher's notes

Each of the 36 Issues includes a set of teacher's notes, including answers.

Issue number

Prerequisites for learning

Lists the prerequisites for learning that children need to have acquired prior to this Issue.

Lists the associated knowledge and skills that contribute to understanding the Issue topic.

Simplifications ⬇

Where appropriate, offers suggestions for supporting children who may be experiencing difficulties understanding the main mathematical ideas.

Extensions ⬆

Where appropriate, offers suggestions for extending children's understanding if you feel they are developing a good understanding of the main mathematical ideas.

Assessment for Learning

Each Issue includes a list of questions specifically designed to assist in assessing pupils' understanding of the Issue topic.

Answers

These are provided where appropriate.

Mathematics topic

Resources

To aid preparation, the resources needed for the Issue are listed.

Teaching support

Provides teaching points for each of the activities in the Issue. These may be helpful when introducing the Issue to the children, or when children experience difficulty whilst working on a particular activity.

Almost all of the activities in *Stretch and Challenge* can be undertaken either individually or in pairs (or sometimes in small groups).

Where an activity is particularly suitable for pairs to work on, this is denoted by 👤 👤.

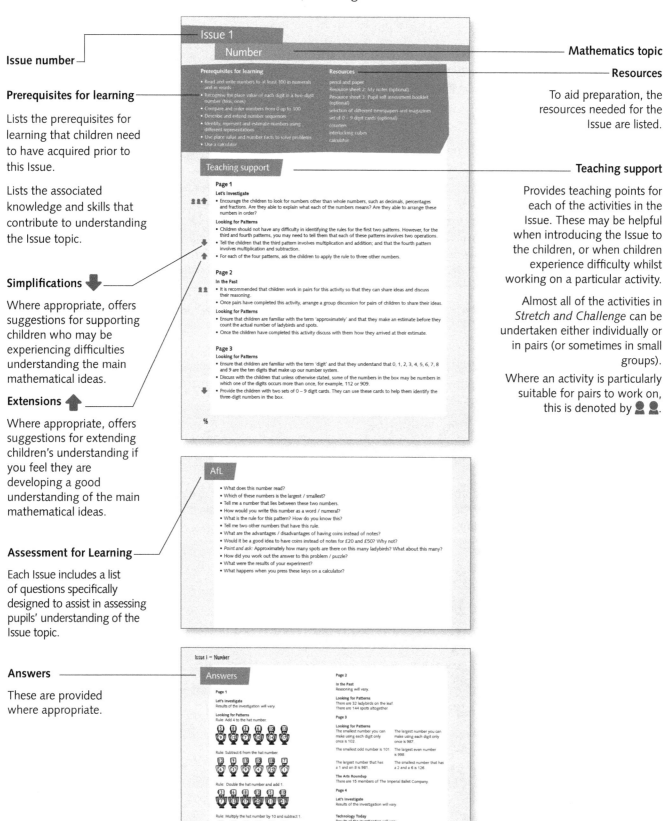

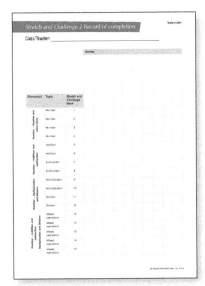

Record of completion

To assist in keeping a record of which Issues children have completed.

Once a child has completed an Issue you could either put a tick or write the date in the corresponding box.

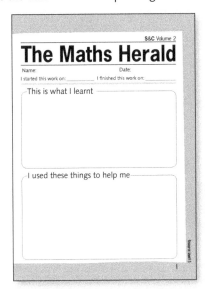

Pupil self assessment booklet

Each Resource Pack in the *Stretch and Challenge* series includes an age-appropriate pupil self assessment A5 booklet (to be printed double sided onto one sheet of A4 paper).

This booklet is a generic sheet that can be used for any, or all, of the 36 Issues in the Resource Pack.

The booklet is designed to provide children with an opportunity to undertake some form of self assessment once they have completed the Issue.

After the children have completed the booklet, discuss with them what they have written.

This can then be kept, together with the child's copy of the Issue and their working out and answers, including, if appropriate, 'My notes'.

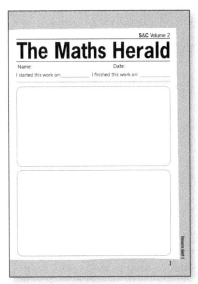

My notes

The pupil activity booklets have been designed to resemble a newspaper. This means that quite often there is insufficient space in the booklets for children to show their working and answers.

You may decide to simply provide children with pencil and paper to record their work or an exercise book that they use as their 'Stretch and Challenge Journal'. Alternatively, you could provide them with a copy of the A5 booklet: 'My notes' (to be printed doubled sided onto one sheet of A4 paper). This can then be kept, together with the child's copy of the Issue and, if appropriate, their 'Pupil self assessment booklet.'

Whichever method you choose for the children to record their working and answers, i.e. on sheets of paper, using a 'My notes' booklet, in an exercise book, or any other method, children need to be clear and systematic in their recording.

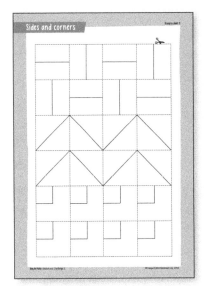

Other Resource sheets

For some of the activities, children are required to use a specific Resource sheet.

These are included both in the back of this Resource Pack and the online resources.

A possible *Stretch and Challenge* teaching and learning sequence

As the diagram on the right illustrates, the process of learning about mathematics can be thought of as the interrelationship between knowledge, understanding and application.

A suggested teaching sequence for working with children based on this model and using the activities in *Stretch and Challenge* is given below.

A complete sequence may occur during a particular lesson if the activity given is designed to be completed during the course of the lesson. Alternatively, the teaching and learning sequence may extend for a longer period of time if the activities are to be completed over the course of several lessons, a week or during a particular unit of work.

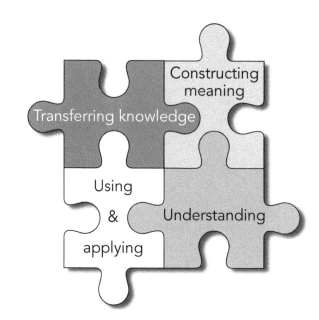

Briefing

The teacher:

- introduces the topic

- checks prerequisites for learning

- introduces the activity including, where appropriate, reading through the activity with the children

- checks for understanding

- clarifies any misconceptions

- ensures there is easy access to any necessary resources.

Working

- Children work individually, in pairs, or if appropriate, in groups.

- Teacher acts only as a 'guide-on-the-side'.

De-briefing

The child / children:

- reports back to others

- reflects on their learning

- identifies the 'next step'.

The teacher evaluates learning.

Links to the Year 2 Mathematics National Curriculum Programme of Study and Attainment Targets

Stretch and Challenge Issue

Number – Number and place value

	1	2	3	4	5	6	7	8	9	10	11	12	13	14	15	16	17	18	19	20	21	22	23	24	25	26	27	28	29	30	31	32	33	34	35	36
count in steps of 2, 3, and 5 from 0, and in tens from any number, forward and backward		•							•	•	•	•																								
recognise the place value of each digit in a two-digit number (tens, ones)		•	•	•																																
identify, represent and estimate numbers using different representations, including the number line		•	•	•																																
compare and order numbers from 0 up to 100; use <, > and = signs		•	•																																	
read and write numbers to at least 100 in numerals and in words		•	•	•	•	•	•	•	•	•	•	•	•	•	•	•	•	•	•	•																
use place value and number facts to solve problems		•	•	•	•	•	•	•	•	•	•	•	•	•	•	•	•	•	•	•																

Notes and guidance (non-statutory)

	1	2	3	4	5	6	7	8	9	10	11	12	13	14	15	16	17	18	19	20	21	22	23	24	25	26	27	28	29	30	31	32	33	34	35	36
Using materials and a range of representations, pupils practise counting, reading, writing and comparing numbers to at least 100 and solving a variety of related problems to develop fluency. They count in multiples of three to support their later understanding of a third.		•	•	•					•	•	•	•	•	•	•	•	•	•	•	•																
As they become more confident with numbers up to 100, pupils are introduced to larger numbers to develop further their recognition of patterns within the number system and represent them in different ways, including spatial representations.		•		•					•	•	•	•	•	•	•	•	•	•	•	•																
Pupils should partition numbers in different ways (for example, 23 = 20 + 3 and 23 = 10 + 13) to support subtraction. They become fluent and apply their knowledge of numbers to reason with, discuss and solve problems that emphasise the value of each digit in two-digit numbers. They begin to understand zero as a place holder.		•																																		

Stretch and Challenge Issue

Number – Addition and subtraction

	1	2	3	4	5	6	7	8	9	10	11	12	13	14	15	16	17	18	19	20	21	22	23	24	25	26	27	28	29	30	31	32	33	34	35	36
• solve problems with addition and subtraction: – using concrete objects and pictorial representations, including those involving numbers, quantities and measures – applying their increasing knowledge of mental and written methods					•	•	•	•				•	•	•	•	•																				
• recall and use addition and subtraction facts to 20 fluently, and derive and use related facts up to 100					•		•	•				•	•	•	•	•																				
• add and subtract numbers using concrete objects, pictorial representations, and mentally, including: – a two-digit number and ones – a two-digit number and tens – two two-digit numbers – adding three one-digit numbers					•		•	•				•	•	•	•	•																				
• show that addition of two numbers can be done in any order (commutative) and subtraction of one number from another cannot						•							•																							
• recognise and use the inverse relationship between addition and subtraction and use this to check calculations and solve missing number problems					•	•	•	•				•	•																							

Notes and guidance (non-statutory)

	1	2	3	4	5	6	7	8	9	10	11	12	13	14	15	16	17	18	19	20	21	22	23	24	25	26	27	28	29	30	31	32	33	34	35	36
Pupils extend their understanding of the language of addition and subtraction to include sum and difference.					•	•	•	•				•	•	•	•	•																				
Pupils practise addition and subtraction to 20 to become increasingly fluent in deriving facts such as using $3 + 7 = 10$; $10 − 7 = 3$ and $7 = 10 − 3$ to calculate $30 + 70 = 100$; $100 − 70 = 30$ and $70 = 100 − 30$. They check their calculations, including adding to check subtraction and adding numbers in a different order to check addition (for example, $5 + 2 + 1 = 1 + 5 + 2 = 1 + 2 + 5$). This establishes commutativity and associativity of addition.					•	•	•	•				•	•	•	•	•																				
Recording addition and subtraction in columns supports place value and prepares for formal written methods with larger numbers.																																				

Stretch and Challenge Issue

Number – Multiplication and division

	1	2	3	4	5	6	7	8	9	10	11	12	13	14	15	16	17	18	19	20	21	22	23	24	25	26	27	28	29	30	31	32	33	34	35	36
• recall and use multiplication and division facts for the 2, 5 and 10 multiplication tables, including recognising odd and even numbers									•	•	•	•	•	•	•																					
• calculate mathematical statements for multiplication and division within the multiplication tables and write them using the multiplication (×), division (÷) and equals (=) signs									•	•	•	•	•	•	•	•																				
• show that multiplication of two numbers can be done in any order (commutative) and division of one number by another cannot									•	•	•	•	•																							
• solve problems involving multiplication and division, using materials, arrays, repeated addition, mental methods, and multiplication and division facts, including problems in contexts									•	•	•	•	•	•	•																					

Notes and guidance (non-statutory)

	1	2	3	4	5	6	7	8	9	10	11	12	13	14	15	16	17	18	19	20	21	22	23	24	25	26	27	28	29	30	31	32	33	34	35	36
Pupils use a variety of language to describe multiplication and division.									•	•	•	•	•	•	•																					
Pupils are introduced to the multiplication tables. They practise to become fluent in the 2, 5 and 10 multiplication tables and connect them to each other. They connect the 10 multiplication table to place value, and the 5 multiplication table to the divisions on the clock face. They begin to use other multiplication tables and recall multiplication facts, including using related division facts to perform written and mental calculations.									•	•	•	•	•	•	•																					
Pupils work with a range of materials and contexts in which multiplication and division relate to grouping and sharing discrete and continuous quantities, to arrays and to repeated addition. They begin to relate these to fractions and measures (for example, $40 \div 2 = 20$, 20 is a half of 40). They use commutativity and inverse relations to develop multiplicative reasoning (for example, $4 \times 5 = 20$ and $20 \div 5 = 4$).									•	•	•	•	•	•	•																					

Stretch and Challenge Issue

Number – Fractions

	1	2	3	4	5	6	7	8	9	10	11	12	13	14	15	16	17	18	19	20	21	22	23	24	25	26	27	28	29	30	31	32	33	34	35	36
recognise, find, name and write fractions $\frac{1}{3}$, $\frac{1}{4}$, $\frac{2}{4}$ and $\frac{3}{4}$ of a length, shape, set of objects or quantity																•		•	•	•	•	•	•													
write simple fractions, for example, $\frac{1}{2}$ of 6 = 3 and recognise the equivalence of $\frac{2}{4}$ and $\frac{1}{2}$																•		•	•																	

Notes and guidance (non-statutory)

	1	2	3	4	5	6	7	8	9	10	11	12	13	14	15	16	17	18	19	20	21	22	23	24	25	26	27	28	29	30	31	32	33	34	35	36
Pupils use fractions as 'fractions of' discrete and continuous quantities by solving problems using shapes, objects and quantities. They connect unit fractions to equal sharing and grouping, to numbers when they can be calculated, and to measures, finding fractions of lengths, quantities, sets of objects or shapes. They meet $\frac{3}{4}$ as the first example of a non-unit fraction.																•		•	•	•	•															
Pupils should count in fractions up to 10, starting from any number and using the $\frac{1}{2}$ and $\frac{2}{4}$ equivalence on the number line (for example, $1\frac{1}{4}$, $1\frac{2}{4}$ (or $1\frac{1}{2}$), $1\frac{3}{4}$, 2). This reinforces the concept of fractions as numbers and that they can add up to more than one.		•														•		•	•	•	•	•	•													

Stretch and Challenge Issue

Measurement

	1	2	3	4	5	6	7	8	9	10	11	12	13	14	15	16	17	18	19	20	21	22	23	24	25	26	27	28	29	30	31	32	33	34	35	36
• choose and use appropriate standard units to estimate and measure length/height in any direction (m/cm); mass (kg/g); temperature (°C); capacity (litres/ml) to the nearest appropriate unit, using rulers, scales, thermometers and measuring vessels																		•			•	•	•	•		•	•									
• compare and order lengths, mass, volume/capacity and record the results using >, < and =																					•	•	•	•		•	•									
• recognise and use symbols for pounds (£) and pence (p); combine amounts to make a particular value								•	•			•	•	•	•	•	•	•																		
• find different combinations of coins that equal the same amounts of money																																				
• solve simple problems in a practical context involving addition and subtraction of money of the same unit, including giving change								•	•			•	•	•	•	•	•	•																		
• compare and sequence intervals of time																						•		•		•										
• tell and write the time to five minutes, including quarter past/to the hour and draw the hands on a clock face to show these times																																				
• know the number of minutes in an hour and the number of hours in a day																								•		•										

Notes and guidance (non-statutory)

	1	2	3	4	5	6	7	8	9	10	11	12	13	14	15	16	17	18	19	20	21	22	23	24	25	26	27	28	29	30	31	32	33	34	35	36
Pupils use standard units of measurement with increasing accuracy, using their knowledge of the number system. They use the appropriate language and record using standard abbreviations.																		•			•	•	•	•		•										
Comparing measures includes simple multiples such as 'half as high'; 'twice as wide'.																				•	•	•														
They become fluent in telling the time on analogue clocks and recording it.																									•											
Pupils become fluent in counting and recognising coins. They read and say amounts of money confidently and use the symbols £ and p accurately, recording pounds and pence separately.								•	•			•	•	•	•	•	•	•	•																	

Stretch and Challenge Issue

Geometry – Properties of shapes

	1	2	3	4	5	6	7	8	9	10	11	12	13	14	15	16	17	18	19	20	21	22	23	24	25	26	27	28	29	30	31	32	33	34	35	36
• identify and describe the properties of 2-D shapes, including the number of sides and line symmetry in a vertical line																											•		•			•	•			
• identify and describe the properties of 3-D shapes, including the number of edges, vertices and faces																												•				•	•			
• identify 2-D shapes on the surface of 3-D shapes, [for example, a circle on a cylinder and a triangle on a pyramid]																												•								
• compare and sort common 2-D and 3-D shapes and everyday objects																										•	•					•	•			

Notes and guidance (non-statutory)

	1	2	3	4	5	6	7	8	9	10	11	12	13	14	15	16	17	18	19	20	21	22	23	24	25	26	27	28	29	30	31	32	33	34	35	36
Pupils handle and name a wide variety of common 2-D and 3-D shapes including: quadrilaterals and polygons, and cuboids, prisms and cones, and identify the properties of each shape (for example, number of sides, number of faces). Pupils identify, compare and sort shapes on the basis of their properties and use vocabulary precisely, such as sides, edges, vertices and faces.																											•	•	•			•				
Pupils read and write names for shapes that are appropriate for their word reading and spelling.																										•	•	•	•			•	•			
Pupils draw lines and shapes using a straight edge.																										•	•	•	•			•	•			

Stretch and Challenge Issue

Geometry – Position and direction

	1	2	3	4	5	6	7	8	9	10	11	12	13	14	15	16	17	18	19	20	21	22	23	24	25	26	27	28	29	30	31	32	33	34	35	36
order and arrange combinations of mathematical objects in patterns and sequences																													•				•			
use mathematical vocabulary to describe position, direction and movement, including movement in a straight line and distinguishing between rotation as a turn and in terms of right angles for quarter, half and three-quarter turns (clockwise and anti-clockwise)																														•	•	•		•		

Notes and guidance (non-statutory)

Pupils should work with patterns of shapes, including those in different orientations.

Pupils use the concept and language of angles to describe 'turn' by applying rotations, including in practical contexts (for example, pupils themselves moving in turns, giving instructions to other pupils to do so, and programming robots using instructions given in right angles).

Statistics

	1	2	3	4	5	6	7	8	9	10	11	12	13	14	15	16	17	18	19	20	21	22	23	24	25	26	27	28	29	30	31	32	33	34	35	36
interpret and construct simple pictograms, tally charts, block diagrams and simple tables																												•				•	•	•	•	•
ask and answer simple questions by counting the number of objects in each category and sorting the categories by quantity																												•				•	•	•	•	•
ask and answer questions about totalling and comparing categorical data																												•				•	•	•	•	•

Notes and guidance (non-statutory)

Pupils record, interpret, collate, organise and compare information (for example, using many-to-one correspondence in pictograms with simple ratios 2, 5, 10).

17

Cross-curricular links to the National Curriculum Programme of Study

Cross-curricular link and *Stretch and Challenge* Feature

Domain(s)	Topic	Issue	Links with home: At Home	Links to money: Money Matters	Physical Education: Sports Update	Design & Technology: Construct	Art & Design / Music: The Arts Roundup	History: In the Past	Geography: Around the World	Computing: Technology Today	Science: Focus on Science	English: The Language of Maths	Mathematics: Let's Investigate	Mathematics: The Puzzler	Mathematics: Looking for Patterns	Mathematics: What's the Problem?
Number: – Number and place value	Number	1					•	•		•			•		•	
	Number	2										•	•		•	
	Number	3	•				•			•		•		•	•	
	Number	4										•	•	•	•	
Number: – Addition and subtraction	Addition	5									•	•	•	•		
	Addition	6					•						•	•	•	
	Subtraction	7											•	•	•	
	Subtraction	8		•						•			•	•		
Number: – Multiplication and division	Multiplication	9		•	•							•	•	•	•	
	Multiplication	10								•			•	•	•	
	Division	11					•						•	•		
	Division	12											•	•		•
Number: – Addition and subtraction	Mixed operations	13		•								•	•	•	•	•
	Mixed operations	14		•		•	•						•	•		
Number: – Multiplication and division	Mixed operations	15		•						•		•		•	•	•
	Mixed operations	16		•						•			•	•	•	•
	Mixed operations	17		•						•			•	•		

Cross-curricular link and *Stretch and Challenge* Feature

Category	Feature	18	19	20	21	22	23	24	25	26	27	28	29	30	31	32	33	34	35	36
Links with home	At Home		•			•	•		•		•			•	•	•	•	•	•	•
Links to money	Money Matters			•																
Physical Education	Sports Update			•	•					•	•								•	•
Design & Technology	Construct	•	•				•	•			•	•		•		•	•			•
Art & Design / Music	The Arts Roundup			•				•										•	•	•
History	In the Past					•														
Geography	Around the World								•	•				•				•	•	
Computing	Technology Today																		•	
Science	Focus on Science					•	•	•			•	•						•		
English	The Language of Maths			•		•	•	•	•	•		•	•	•	•	•	•	•	•	•
Mathematics	Let's Investigate	•	•	•		•	•	•	•		•		•	•		•		•	•	•
	The Puzzler		•	•		•				•	•		•	•	•	•	•			
	Looking for Patterns	•									•				•					
	What's the Problem?	•		•		•		•	•	•										

Issue	Topic	Domain(s)
18	Fractions	Number: – Fractions
19	Fractions	
20	Fractions	
21	Length and height	Measurement
22	Mass	
23	Capacity and volume	
24	Time	
25	Measurement	
26	Measurement	
27	2-D shapes	Geometry: – Properties of shapes
28	3-D shapes	
29	Symmetry	
30	Position and direction	Geometry: – Position and direction
31	Movement and angle	
32	Geometry	Geometry: – Properties of shapes
33	Geometry	– Position and direction
34	Statistics	Statistics
35	Statistics	
36	Statistics	

Resources used in *Stretch and Challenge 2*

A fundamental skill of mathematics is knowing what resources to use and when it is appropriate to use them. It is for this reason that many of the activities in *Stretch and Challenge 2* give no indication to the children as to which resources to use. Although the teacher's notes that accompany each activity include a list of resources, children should be encouraged to work out for themselves what they will need to use to successfully complete an activity.

It is assumed that for each activity children will have ready access to pencil and paper, and any other resources that are specifically mentioned in an activity, for example, computers or other Resource sheets. However, all other equipment should be left for the children to locate and use as and when they see is appropriate.

A list of all the resources children are likely to need in *Stretch and Challenge 2* is given below.

Resource	Stretch and Challenge Issue																	
	1	2	3	4	5	6	7	8	9	10	11	12	13	14	15	16	17	18
pencil and paper	•	•	•	•	•	•	•	•	•	•	•	•	•	•	•	•	•	•
Resource sheets	2, 3	2, 3, 21, 22	2, 3, 4, 5, 19	2, 3, 6, 19, 20	2, 3, 6, 20	2, 3	2, 3	2, 3	2, 3, 7, 20	2, 3, 6	2, 3, 20	2, 3	2, 3	2, 3	2, 3	2, 3	2, 3, 8	2, 3, 9, 10, 19, 20
computer with internet access			•										•					
ruler				•	•													•
scissors								•									•	•
calculator	•		•	•						•	•		•	•	•		•	
counters	•	•		•		•		•		•	•	•				•	•	
interlocking cubes	•												•					•
selection of different newspapers and magazines	•		•															
0 – 9 digit cards	•	•	•	•		•	•	•	•		•							
A3 paper		•																
coloured pencils				•					•	•								•
square pieces of paper; modelling clay; weighing scales / balance; non-transparent bag or box																		•
set of 1 – 100 number cards (or Resource sheet 4); simple percussion instrument, e.g. triangle, chime bar, hand bell, …			•															
stopwatch				•														
set of dominoes						•												
1 – 6 dice						•	•						•					
art paper						•												
5p, 10p, 20p, 50p coins (real or play)									•									
pot / container													•					
20 x £1 coins (real or play) or counters															•			
5p, 10p, 20p, 50p, £1, £2 coins (real or play)														•				
selection of coins (real or play); several different mobile phones																	•	

Resource	Stretch and Challenge Issue																	
	19	20	21	22	23	24	25	26	27	28	29	30	31	32	33	34	35	36
pencil and paper	•	•	•	•	•	•	•	•	•	•	•	•	•	•	•	•	•	•
Resource sheets	2, 3, 9, 11	2, 3	2, 3	2, 3	2, 3	2, 3	2, 3	2, 3, 19, 20	2, 3, 7, 12, 13, 21	2, 3	2, 3, 14, 15	2, 3, 16, 20	2, 3	2, 3, 17	2, 3, 18, 19, 20, 21	2, 3, 19, 20	2, 3, 19, 20	2, 3
computer						•		•								•	•	
computer with internet access															•			
data handling software								•								•	•	
ruler	•					•		•	•			•	•	•	•	•	•	•
scissors	•					•		•	•			•	•	•		•		
calculator		•	•															
counters					•						•	•	•					
interlocking cubes			•	•	•					•								
selection of coins (real or play); several different mobile phones																		
matchsticks; geoboards and elastic bands									•									
football; piece of chalk or some small stickers; junk such as cardboard boxes and other modelling material; Lego pieces										•								
coloured pencils	•				•						•	•	•					
mirror											•							
large world map													•					
scrap of paper; A4 paper														•				
circle geometric shape; camera; three paper squares, preferably each a different colour															•			
newspaper or magazine showing television listings						•									•			
square sheet of paper; matchsticks; compass															•			
individual and group skipping rope; stick				•														
trundle wheel; tape measure		•	•				•											
kitchen scales, bathroom scales; balance; 500 g ($\frac{1}{2}$ kg) weight; container of pennies; container of marbles; 0 – 9 dice				•														
large clear plastic calibrated measuring jug half full of water, e.g. 1 or 2 litre jug; collection of waterproof objects that will fit into the measuring jug; selection of containers ranging from less than 0·5 litres to over 2 litres; cup; range of different containers larger than the cup, e.g. jugs, bottles, yoghurt pots; access to water; funnel; selection of different commercially available construction materials						•												
stopwatch; material for constructing a 1 minute sand timer, i.e. plastic bottle, sand, sticky tape; calendar; markers							•											
large sheet of paper							•	•									•	
ball; several sheets of paper of differing sizes; 6 hard-boiled eggs; daily newspaper for one week							•											
thermometer; selection of newspapers and magazines; analogue clock								•										
glue								•									•	
toy car; apparatus to make slopes where the incline and surface can be changed; small weight to attach to the toy car; counting apparatus, e.g. counters, beads, cubes; containers																•		
selection of travel brochures and magazines; material for making a poster; white pages telephone directory																	•	
circular pieces of paper; selection of fruit such as tangerines, satsumas, clementines, oranges; plate	•																	

Introduction

The Issues start on the next page.

The Maths Herald

Name: _____

Date: _____

Let's Investigate

Look through some newspapers and magazines.
Find as many different numbers as you can.

Find both numerals  **4** and words. 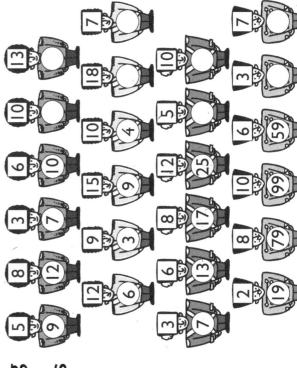 **six**

Cut them out.

Put your numbers in order, smallest to largest.

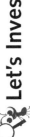 Looking for Patterns

Find the rule that links the number on the hat to the number on the coat. Write in the missing numbers.

 Let's Investigate

Approximately how many counters can you hold in your hand?

How many interlocking cubes can you hold in your hand?

Can you hold more counters or more cubes?

Can you hold twice as much, more than twice as much or less than twice as much in two hands?

Write down what you think.

Now find out.

Technology Today

Press these keys on a calculator:

5 **+** **=** **=**

Keep pressing the **=** key.

What do you notice?

What happens when you press these keys?

3 **+** **2** **=** **=**

Investigate using different pairs of numbers.

Investigate what happens when the first number is a 2-digit or 3-digit number and you press the subtraction sign.

8 **5** **–** **5** **=** **=**

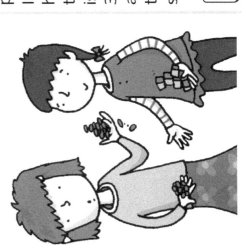

In the Past

In the UK, £1 notes were once used, but now we use £1 coins.

What do you think is better?

Why?

Looking for Patterns

Estimate how many ladybirds are on this leaf.

Each ladybird has 3, 4, 5 or 6 spots on their back.

Approximately how many spots are there altogether?

Now count them.

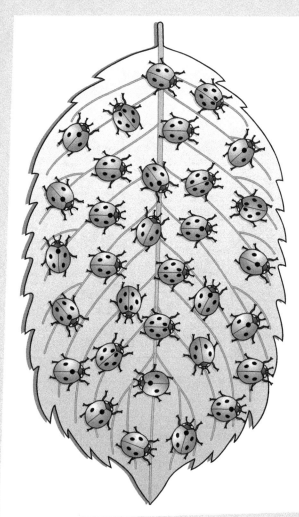

Looking for Patterns

What 3-digit numbers are in the box?

I'm the smallest number you can make using each digit only once.

I'm the smallest odd number.

I'm the largest number that has a 1 and an 8.

I'm the largest number you can make using each digit only once.

I'm the largest even number.

I'm the smallest number that has a 2 and a 6.

THREE-DIGIT NUMBERS ONLY (All other numbers KEEP OUT)

The Arts Roundup

The Imperial Ballet Company dancers stand in a line waiting to go on stage.

Polly sees that she is 8th from the front of the line and also 8th from the back of the line.

How many people are in the line?

approximation

The Maths Herald

Name:

Date:

🐜 Let's Investigate

3-digit numbers where the
sum of the digits is 4.

$1 + 1 + 2 = 4$

112

I can make 12 different

Is Conroy right?

🐜 Let's Investigate

How many children in your
class can stand on a large
(A3) sheet of paper at the
same time?

Everyone must have both
feet on the paper!

How many sheets would
you need for everyone in
your class?

🐜 Looking for Patterns

Without counting, write the letters
of each shape in order, starting with
the shape that you think has the
most dots in it.

Most
dots

Least
dots

Now estimate how many dots are
inside each shape.

A   B   C   D   E

🐜 Let's Investigate

Look at Shape D in the
Looking for Patterns
activity above.

Using squared dot paper,
draw a different shape that
has about the same number
of dots inside it.

Draw other shapes with
approximately this number
of dots inside them.

Compare your sheet with a
friend's. Without counting,
which shapes do you think
have more dots?

Which shapes
have fewer
dots?

Count them
and see
if you
are right.

4

Looking for Patterns

Find the rule and write the next three numbers.

25 22 19 16

$\frac{1}{2}$ 1 $1\frac{1}{2}$ 2

0 1 4 9

3 11 19 27

1 2 4 7

20 19 17 16 14

The Language of Maths

Lisa, Gary and John are friends.
Their ages are 8, 9 and 10.
Lisa is not the youngest.
John is older than Gary.
Lisa's age is an even number.
How old is each friend?

digit

Looking for Patterns

This is a 1–100 number square, but not as you know it!

1	2	3	4	5	6	7	8	9	10
20	19	18	17	16	15	14	13	12	11
21	22	23	24	25	26	27	28	29	30
40	39	38	37	36	35	34	33	32	31

?

??

Find the numbers that belong in the ? and ?? squares.

Can you find ? and ?? without numbering all the blank squares?

What patterns do you notice?

Looking for Patterns

The 1st triangle is made from 3 counters.

The 2nd triangle is made from 6 counters.

How many counters do you need to make the 3rd triangle? Draw it.

Now draw the 4th and 5th triangles.

Write down the 5 numbers for how many counters there are in each triangle.

These numbers have a special name. Find out what it is.

The Maths Herald

Name:

Date:

Technology Today

A calculator uses 7 light bars to make each of the digits from 0 to 9.

The number 2 uses 5 light bars.

Draw each of the other digits from 0 to 9 in digital form using light bars.

How many light bars are used to make each of the digits?

Looking for Patterns

Work with a friend.

Sort a set of 1–100 number cards and write about how you sorted them.

How else can you sort the cards?

Sort the cards in as many different ways as you can think of.

The Language of Maths

Look through a newspaper.

How many of these pages are about:

- news?
- sport?

How many have:

- ads?
- photos?
- drawings?

How many show:

- graphs?
- tables?

What else can you find out about the paper?

Do you think this is the same for all newspapers?

Find out!

The Puzzler

Shuffle a pack of 0–9 digit cards and place them face down in a pile.

Take the top card and place it face up on one of the blank cards on the sheet.

Do this 6 times altogether.

Once a digit card is placed on a blank card it cannot be moved.

The object of the puzzle is to get all 6 cards in order, smallest to largest. Something like this:

Six card puzzle

| 0 | 1 | 3 | 5 | 6 | 8 |

Good luck!

Try the puzzle several times.

Do you get better each time?

The Arts Roundup

Rhythm is the repeated pattern of sound or movement. It is very important to musicians and dancers.

Create a simple rhythm using sound. Record your rhythm so that others in the class can perform your tune.

Think carefully about how you are going to record your tune and what symbols you are going to use.

The Language of Maths

Look at these words.

- triple
- trio
- tricycle
- triathlon
- tripod
- triplets

What do they all have in common? What do you think this means?

order

The Puzzler

0 1 2 3 4 5 6 7 8 9 10

ZERO = 4
ONE = 3
TWO = 3
THREE = 5

What does FOUR equal!? What about FIVE, SIX, SEVEN, EIGHT, NINE and TEN?

Write about how you worked out the value of the numbers.

At Home

Who in your family do you think makes the most telephone calls in a week? Find out!

Make a list of everyone who lives in your house.

Put the list beside the telephone and tell everyone to put a tally mark beside their name when they make a phone call.

Mum	＃＃ ((((
Dad	＃＃ (
Simon	(((
Susan	＃＃ ((

Don't forget about mobile phone calls or calls made at work. You may want to give everyone in your family a piece of paper to use to keep a record of all their other calls, or ask them to remember and make tally marks on your list. Remember, you need to keep a record of all the phone calls made in a week.

© HarperCollinsPublishers 2016

The Maths Herald

Name:

Date:

prediction

Let's Investigate

A **palindrome** is a word or number that reads the same backwards as forwards.

For example, 'ANNA', 'TOOT', 55, 202 and 373.

There are 9 palindromes between 10 and 100. Write them here.

There are 10 palindromes between 100 and 200. Write them here.

There are 10 palindromes between 200 and 300. Write them here.

Look at all the palindromes between 100 and 300. What pattern do you notice?

Can you continue this pattern to find all the palindromes from 300 to 1000?

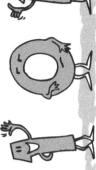

Looking for Patterns

Imagine you are going to draw a large 1–100 number square with chalk on the school playground.

To write the number 26 you would write the digit **2** and the digit **6**.

How many of each digit would you write to make the 1–100 number square?

Write about what you did.

Remember!
The digits are:
0, 1, 2, 3, 4, 5, 6, 7, 8 and 9.

The Puzzler

Take a set of 0–9 digit cards and some counters.

Shuffle the cards and lay them face up in a line. For example:

9 5 3 8 2 6 0 1 7 4

Swap two cards and take a counter.

9 2 3 8 5 6 0 1 7 4

Keep swapping pairs of cards and taking a counter, until all the cards are in order from 0 to 9.

0 1 2 3 4 5 6 7 8 9

Count the number of counters.

Try the puzzle several times.

Are you getting better? If you get fewer counters, you are.

Good luck!

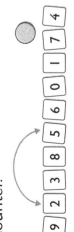

The Language of Maths

Work with a friend.

You are each going to write down your first and last names as many times as possible in one minute.

Who do you think will write their name more times? Why?

Now find out. Use a stopwatch or the seconds hand on a clock to time each other.

Was your prediction correct?

What would be the result if you both wrote down the same name, perhaps the name of your teacher? Why do you think this?

Investigate.

The Puzzler

Draw a ring around any group of three numbers that are in order, smallest to largest.

The numbers must go left to right →, or top to bottom ↓.

Every number is part of a group.

Two have been done for you.

17	9	18	22	10	28
23	2	51	60	33	71
45	42	49	83	40	99
31	28	35	32	46	67
85	55	45	13	42	80
93	71	62	50	51	53

Looking for Patterns

Look at this pattern:

Using squared paper, draw shapes 5, 6 and 7.

Count the number of squares in each shape and write them in the table.

Shape number	1	2	3	4	5	6	7	8	9	10
Number of squares										

Look at the table. Can you work out how many squares there will be in shapes 8, 9 and 10?

The Puzzler

Place 12 counters on this grid so that each column ↕ and row ↔ has an even number of counters.

Here is one way:

How many ways can you do this?

Draw each of the different ways on 2 cm squared paper.

S&C Volume 2

The Maths Herald

Name:

Date:

total

Focus on Science

6 animals are standing in a field.

How many legs do they have altogether?

Write a number sentence about them and how many legs there are.

Think of 6 different animals in the field that have the **same** total number of legs.

Write a number sentence about them and how many legs there are.

Now think of 6 different animals in the field that have a **different** total number of legs.

Write a number sentence that has a **different** total number of legs.

Write a number sentence that has a different number of legs altogether.

The Puzzler

These puzzles are similar to The Puzzler activity on page 3.

However, each symbol stands for a different number.

How much is each symbol worth?

Show your solutions on 2 cm squared paper.

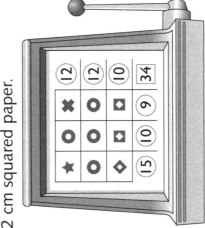

The Puzzler

Play this version of Noughts and Crosses with a friend.

Instead of one player using noughts ◯ and the other player using crosses ✕, use these odd and even numbers.

Odd	Even
1, 3, 5, 7, 9	2, 4, 6, 8, 10

Rules:

- Decide who is odd and who is even.

- You can only use each number once in a game.

- The winner is the first player to make a total of 15.

Play 4 games, taking turns to be odds and evens.

After you have played 4 games, discuss strategies for winning the game with your friend.

Let's Investigate

Choose any number on a 1–100 number square.

- Add the 2 numbers to its left.
- Add the 2 numbers below it.
- Find the difference.

Do this several times. What do you notice?

Now choose any number on the 1–100 square.

- Add the 3 numbers to its left.
- Add the 3 numbers below it.
- Find the difference.

Do this several times.
What do you notice?

1	2	3	4	5	6	7	8	9	10
11	12	13	14	15	16	17	18	19	20
21	22	23	24	25	26	27	28	29	30
31	32	33	34	35	36	37	38	39	40
41	42	43	44	45	46	47	48	49	50
51	52	53	54	55	56	57	58	59	60
61	62	63	64	65	66	67	68	69	70
71	72	73	74	75	76	77	78	79	80
81	82	83	84	85	86	87	88	89	90
91	92	93	94	95	96	97	98	99	100

Let's Investigate

Choose any number on a 1–100 number square.

Add the numbers on either side.

Do this several times. What do you notice?

Now choose any number on a 1–100 number square and add the eight numbers that surround it.

Do this several times. What do you notice?

1	2	3
11	12	13
21	22	23

1	2	3
11	12	13
21	22	23

The Language of Maths

M I C H A E L
13 + 9 + 3 + 8 + 1 + 5 + 12 = 51

Each letter of the alphabet is worth points.

A is worth 1 point. B is worth 2 points.

C is worth 3 points, and so on.

Draw a table to show what each letter is worth.

What is your name worth?

Who in your class do you think has the most points?

What about the least points? Find out.

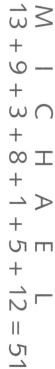

F = 6
E = 5
D = 4
C = 3
B = 2
A = 1

The Puzzler

Add the numbers in each row and column and write the answers in the circles.

Then add the numbers in the circles in each row and column, and write the final answer in the empty box.

What do you notice?

8	5	○
4	7	○
○	○	□

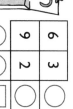

6	3	○
9	2	○
○	○	□

12	4	○
6	7	○
○	○	□

Now try these.

7	(10)
5	(17)
□	□

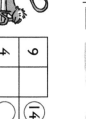

4	(14)
2	3	(10)

9	(14)
4	(16)

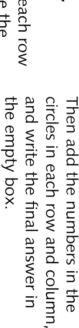

The Maths Herald

Name:

Date:

The Puzzler

Write either a 4 or a 5 in the empty boxes to complete each number sentence.

☐ + ☐ = 9

2 ☐ + 2 = ☐ 0

1 ☐ + 9 = ☐ 2

☐ 2 + ☐ 1 = 93

2 ☐ + ☐ 2 = 67

3 + ☐ 2 = ☐ 8

Looking for Patterns

Write this number sentence in a different order to make it easier to add.

$8 + 7 + 2 + 3 + 5$

Now do the same to these number sentences.

$9 + 5 + 3 + 11 + 5$

$12 + 6 + 8 + 7 + 4$

Why are they now easier?

number sentence

Let's Investigate

1 | 3 | 4 | 5 | 6 | 7 | 8 | 9

3
4
5
6
7

1
2
5
8
9

Arrange all the digits 1 to 9 so that both lines of 5 numbers add up to the same total.

Here is one way.

How many different ways can you do this?

The Arts Roundup

Use these shapes to draw 3 different pictures, each to the value of exactly £1.

You must use each shape at least once.

Here is one to get you started.

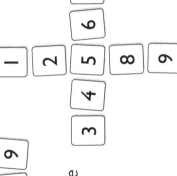
I'm worth 5p.

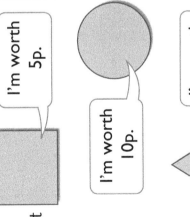
I'm worth 10p.

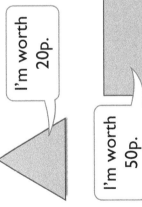
I'm worth 20p.

I'm worth 50p.

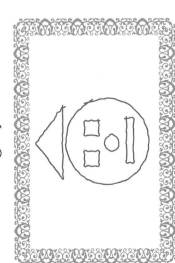

The Puzzler

40   41   42   43   44   46

15   18   16   19   17   14

29   24   26   23   28   27

Draw lines matching a boat number with a ball number so that when each pair of numbers are added together they make one of the numbers on the huts above.

Let's Investigate

How many pairs of numbers can you find in this grid that total 100? What about 3 numbers that add together to total 100?

16	30	25	80	76	32
10	42	40	39	51	45
24	57	62	87	34	20
13	11	50	46	90	61
68	60	84	38	43	35
23	75	49	70	14	50

Let's Investigate

Use a set of dominoes.

How many different groups of dominoes can you make that have a total of 24 dots?

Here are two groups to get you started.

Looking for Patterns

The total of the 3 numbers on the **top** of these dice is 11.

The total of the 3 numbers on the **bottom** of these dice is 10.

What is the total of the 3 numbers on the **top** of these dice?

The total of the 3 numbers on the **top** of these dice is 7.

The total of the 3 numbers on the **bottom** of these dice is 14.

What is the total of the 3 numbers on the **bottom** of these dice?

What is the total of the 3 numbers on the **top** of each group?

What is the total of the 3 numbers on the **bottom** of each group?

How did you work out the answers?

The Maths Herald

Name: _____ Date: _____

Looking for Patterns

$2\,\star - 6 = 1\,\star$ $1\,\star - 9 = \star\,0$

$1\,\star - \star = 9$ $57 - 2\,\star = \star\,1$

$29 - \star\,\star = 4$

(rockets numbered) 0 1 2 3 4 5 6 7 8 9

Write the digits 0–9 to complete these number sentences.

You can only use each digit once.

Hint: Before you start, look carefully at all 5 number sentences. Which one should you begin with?

How did you work out the missing digits?

The Puzzler

(digits in clouds) 1 3 5 7 9
2 4 6 8

odd   odd
odd   odd   odd
odd   odd   odd
ppo   ppo

Write a digit in each circle.

The difference between the 2 numbers joined by a line must be odd.

Like this: 8 —odd— 3

$(8 - 3 = 5)$

5 is an odd number.

You can only use each digit once.

Can you find more than one way of doing this?

Let's Investigate

For this activity you need 2 1–6 dice and some counters.

Roll the 2 dice.

Work out the difference between the 2 numbers.

$6 - 2 = 4$

12	16

Place counters on 2 numbers that have the same difference.

Keep going until you have placed a counter on each number.

10	15	6	13
14	3	18	9
7	17	12	4
5	11	8	16

Now, with a friend, talk about how you could make this into a paired game.

Play the game.

If you need to, change your rules to make the best game possible.

difference

The Puzzler

| 21 | 22 | 23 | 24 | 25 | 27 |

| 37 | 39 | 34 | 36 | 38 | 35 |

| 13 | 15 | 11 | 10 | 16 | 12 |

Draw lines matching a shirt number with a shorts number so that when one number is subtracted from the other number, the answer makes one of the numbers on the cupboards above.

Let's Investigate

| 1 | 2 | 3 | 4 | 5 |
| 6 | 7 | 8 | 9 |

2-digit numbers and find the difference between the pairs of numbers.

$$\Box - \Box = \,?$$

How many different subtraction number sentences can you make?

Choose any 3 cards from a set of 1–9 digit cards.

Arrange the 3 cards into different pairs of 1-digit and digit cards.

Repeat, choosing 3 different digit cards.

Let's Investigate

① ② ③ ④ ⑤ ⑥ ⑦ ⑧ ⑨

$$\Box - \Box = \bigcirc\bigcirc$$

Replace □ and ○ with digits to make different subtraction number sentences.

Here is one:
43 – 26 = 17

□ stands for an even digit.

○ stands for an odd digit.

The Puzzler

Start at 20. Find a path to each diamond. Subtract each number you land on as you move.

You can only move up or down or left or right (not diagonally).

Write each final number in the diamond ◇.

Now give your sheet to a friend.

Can they work out what numbers you landed on?

One has been done for you.

20 – 1 – 3 – 6 = 10

The Maths Herald

Name:

Date:

Money Matters

Using only these coins, investigate which amounts up to £1 can be made using 1, 2, 3 or all of these coins.

What is the change from £1 for each amount?

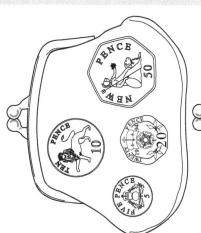

Record your results in a table. Here are 2 to get you started.

Coins	Amount	Change from £1
5p, 10p	15p	85p
5p, 10p, 20p	35p	65p

The Puzzler

There are 4 numbers in the box. They are all more than 10 and less than 50. What are the 4 numbers?

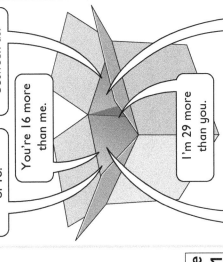

There is a difference of 13 between us.

2 of us have a difference of 18.

You're 16 more than me.

I'm 29 more than you.

One of us is 11 less than another.

We have a difference of 5.

Could they be other numbers?

Let's Investigate

1	2	3	4	5

6	7	8	9

Choose any 4 cards from a set of 1–9 digit cards.

Arrange the 4 cards to make different pairs of 2-digit numbers and find the difference between each pair.

☐☐ – ☐☐ = ☐☐

How many different subtraction calculations can you make?

Repeat, choosing 4 different digit cards.

Money Matters

If you spend just 1 coin from each of these purses, what are the different amounts you could have left?

change (money)

Technology Today

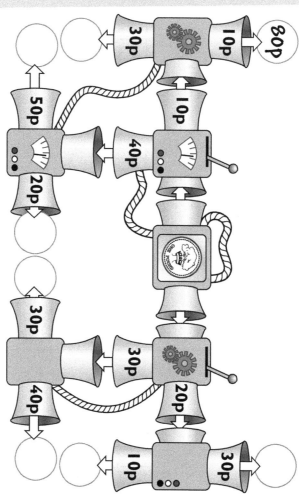

Start at the £1 coin.

As the £1 coin moves through the machine it loses value.

Write each final amount of money in the circles.

One has been done for you.

The Puzzler

$$CD - C = P$$

What digit does each of the letters stand for?

How did you work out the values of C, D and P?

The Puzzler

Write either a 2 or a 3 in the empty boxes to complete each number sentence.

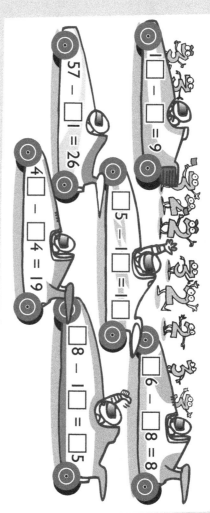

$$\square - \square = 9$$

$$57 - \square 1 = 26$$

$$4\square - \square 4 = 19$$

$$\square 5 - 1\square = \square$$

$$8 - 1\square = \square 5$$

$$6 - \square 8 = 8$$

Let's Investigate

Use a set of 0–9 digit cards, a subtraction card and an equals card.

| 0 | 1 | 2 | 3 | 4 | 5 |

| 6 | 7 | 8 | 9 | – | = |

How many different subtraction number sentences can you make that all use the [5] card?

Here are 3 to get you started.

$$9 - 5 = 4$$

$$8 - 3 = 5$$

$$9 - 5 = 4$$

$$8 - 3 = 5$$

$$5 - 4 = 1$$

What if all the number sentences used the [9] card?

© HarperCollinsPublishers 2016

The Maths Herald

Name: _____

Date: _____

The Puzzler

Baskets: 34, 48, 52, 84, 90, 120

Balloons: 14, 17, 15, 18, 16, 13

Sacks: 2, 4, 6, 3, 5, 8

Draw lines matching a balloon number with a basket number so that when one number is multiplied by the other number, the answer makes one of the numbers above.

Let's Investigate

3 6 9

4 8 12

5 10 15

Continue these lists of the multiples of 3 and 4.

Which numbers are in both lists? What do you notice about these numbers?

Continue this list of the multiples of 5. Which numbers are in the multiples of 3 list and the multiples of 5 list?

© HarperCollinsPublishers 2016

1

Looking for Patterns

START	30	45	15	73	35	97	2	22	85
40	10	86	3	41	94	59	50	34	19
16	58	29	21	33	27	71	13	65	38
32	4	56	77	17	6	46	82	11	37
31	67	44	34	55	39	48	9	36	12
26	5	24	20	64	79	95	43	41	42
14	70	89	74	48	94	7	83	10	24
82	25	49	98	8	38	5	22	61	18
11	53	17	86	36	47	50	77	26	51
27	91	23	62	12	52	28	60	68	END

Look at this grid. It is possible to move from START to END only landing on squares that are multiples of 3.

You can only move sideways ↔ or up and down ↕, not diagonally.

Colour the squares to show the path.

It is also possible to move from START to END only landing on squares that are multiples of 4.

Colour the squares to show the path.

Use a different colour to show the path.

multiple

Looking for Patterns

2 cm squared paper

START

END

Using 2 cm squared paper, design your own multiples puzzle similar to that in the Looking for Patterns activity above.

Write your puzzle for multiples of 3 and multiples of 5.

Remember, you can only move sideways ↔ or up and down ↕, not diagonally.

4

Sports Update

Look at the numbers on each of the cars on this racing track. These are the cars' starting points.

Every time a car drives over a chequered strip it doubles its points.

Every time a car drives under a bridge it loses 1 point.

Work out the final score for each car.

Let's Investigate

Using a set of 0–9 digit cards, investigate making pairs of numbers so that one number is 2 times the other number.

Here are 3 examples:

4	8

8	6	1	2

4	1	2

0	1	2	3	4
5	6	7	8	9

1	4	2	8

What about using the cards to make pairs of numbers so that one number is 3 times the other number?

What about using the cards to make pairs of numbers so that one number is 4 times the other number?

Let's Investigate

Look at the tile pattern on the sheet.

Write a multiplication number sentence that describes how many square tiles there are.

Now cut out all the squares. How many different rectangles can you make by rearranging the 24 squares?

Write a multiplication number sentence for each one.

What different rectangles can you make by rearranging fewer than 24 squares?

Write a multiplication number sentence for each one.

Money Matters

Madeline, Cathy, Coleen, Jill and Peter are friends.

They put all their pocket money together to buy a computer game that they can share.

Cathy has £2.

Coleen has twice the amount of money that Jill has. Jill has twice the amount of money that Cathy has. Peter has £2 more than Jill.

Madeline has the rest.

How much money do Madeline, Coleen, Jill and Peter have?

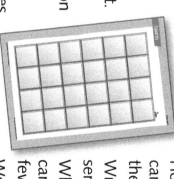

£30

The Maths Herald

Name:

Date:

🐜 Looking for Patterns

On one of the 1–100 number squares on the sheet, colour all the multiples of 2.

What pattern do you notice?

Use the other 3 1–100 number squares on the sheet to:

- colour all the multiples of 3
- colour all the multiples of 4
- colour all the multiples of 5.

What patterns do you notice?

🐜 Looking for Patterns

Continue to write out the 2 multiplication table.

How can you use the 2 multiplication table to help you with the 4 multiplication table?

$$1 \times 2 = 2$$
$$2 \times 2 = 4$$
$$3 \times 2 = 6$$
$$4 \times 2 = 8$$

🐜 The Puzzler

Write either a 2 or a 5 in the empty boxes to complete each number sentence.

☐ × ☐ = 10

1 × ☐ = 30

☐ × 10 = 0

1 × ☐ = 60

1 × 8 = 1 ☐ 0

☐ × ☐ = 0

🐜 Technology Today

2 3 5 × =

Using only the above keys on a calculator it is possible to make the following number sentences.

2 × 3 = 6

2 5 × 3 = 75

What other number sentences can you make?

You can only press a key once in each number sentence.

Let's Investigate

Write different number sentences using only these numbers and signs.

Looking for Patterns

Look at the sheet you made in the first 🏁 **Looking for Patterns** activity on page 1.

On the 100 square with all the multiples of 2 coloured, draw a ring around all the multiples of 3. What patterns do you notice?

On the 100 square with all the multiples of 3 coloured, draw a ring around all the multiples of 4. What patterns do you notice?

On the 100 square with all the multiples of 4 coloured, draw a ring around all the multiples of 5. What patterns do you notice?

On the 100 square with all the multiples of 5 coloured, draw a ring around all the multiples of 3. What patterns do you notice?

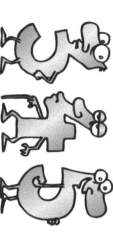

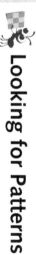

Looking for Patterns

The table below can show all the multiplication tables up to 10 × 10.

The column ↕ and row ↔ for the 1 multiplication table has been done for you – they are so easy!

You should know by heart the 2, 5 and 10 multiplication tables.

Complete these columns ↕ and rows ↔ on the grid. They are shaded grey.

What about the 3 and 4 multiplication tables? Complete these rows ↔ and columns ↕ on the grid.

> common multiple

So, this leaves just these 16 multiplication tables facts.

Look at the pattern in each column ↕ and row ↔ and complete the grid.

×	1	2	3	4	5	6	7	8	9	10
1	1	2	3	4	5	6	7	8	9	10
2	2									
3	3									
4	4									
5	5									
6	6									
7	7									
8	8									
9	9									
10	10									

Now you know the answers to all the multiplication tables up to 10 × 10. Well done!

S&C Volume 2

The Maths Herald

Name:

Date:

The Arts Roundup

Elton Choir have made biscuits to sell as a fund raising event.

They are selling them in bags of 24 biscuits because that way they can be shared out fairly by different-sized groups of people.

What sized groups could share the 24 biscuits evenly?

The Language of Maths

Always, sometimes, never true?

Is Michael's statement always true, sometimes true or never true?

Explain your decision.

> If a number can be divided by 2 and by 5, then it can also be divided by 10.

divisible

Let's Investigate

The numbers in this list can all be divided by 3.

6
9
12    $1 + 2 = 3$
15    $1 + 5 = 6$
18    $1 + 8 = 9$
21    $2 + 1 = 3$

If you add the 2 digits of the 2-digit numbers together the answer can also be divided by 3.

Investigate other numbers which can be divided by 3.

Can the sum of their digits be divided by 3?

Let's Investigate

Using a set of 0–9 digit cards, investigate making 2-digit numbers which can be divided by 3.

Here are 3 examples:

1 8   2 4   3 0

0 1 2 3 4
5 6 7 8 9

What about using the cards to make 2-digit numbers that can be divided by 4?

The Puzzler

Write either a 2 or a 4 in the empty boxes to complete each number sentence.

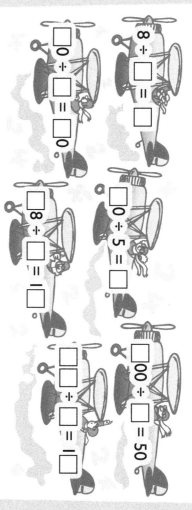

$8 \div \square = \square$

$\square \div \square = 0$

$0 \div 5 = \square$

$\square 8 \div \square = I$

$\square 00 \div \square = 50$

$\square \div \square = I$

Let's Investigate

You need:

- 30 counters
- sheet of 2 cm squared paper

Using 10 counters it is possible to make this rectangle.

Using 12 counters it is possible to make these 2 rectangles.

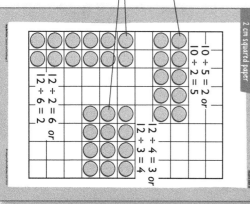

2 cm squared paper

$10 \div 5 = 2$ or
$10 \div 2 = 5$

$12 \div 2 = 6$ or
$12 \div 6 = 2$

$12 \div 4 = 3$ or
$12 \div 3 = 4$

What rectangles can you make using other numbers of counters?

Write the division number sentence for each rectangle.

Let's Investigate

How many paving stones are there on this path?

Imagine writing your first name over and over again, one letter on each stone, until all the stones have a letter on them.

How many times do you think you would write your name completely?

Why do you think this?

Now try it out.

Did your name fit exactly the number of stones?

Can you think of someone else who would be able to write their name over and over again fitting exactly the number of stones?

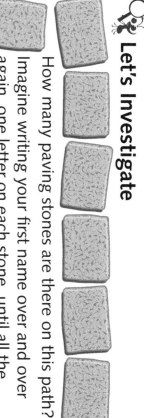

The Puzzler

Cross out 2 numbers from this grid so that the total of the remaining numbers in each row ↔ and column ↕ divide exactly by 5.

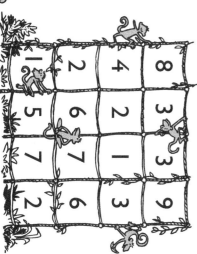

8	3	3	9
4	2	1	3
2	6	7	6
1	5	7	2

S&C Volume 2

The Maths Herald

Name:

Date:

What's the Problem?

Mario has 36 eggs. He wants to give them all away to his friends, but only if each person gets the same number of eggs.

How many different ways can he do this?

The Puzzler

Look at this train.

Each carriage number is half the previous carriage number. The last carriage is an odd number.

It is a 4-carriage train.

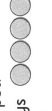

24 12 6 3

Make your own trains. Start with a 2-digit even number. Keep halving until you reach an odd number.

Can you make a 3-carriage train?

Can you make another 4-carriage train?

What about a 5-carriage train?

What is the longest train you can make starting with a 2-digit number?

Let's Investigate

Roll the dice.

Find a division number sentence with that answer and cover it with a counter.

$$20 \div 5 = 4$$

Take a cube out of the pot.

Repeat until you make a line of 5 counters.

A line can be sideways, up or down or diagonal.

You need:
- 1–6 dice
- counters
- pot of cubes

How many cubes did you take out of the pot?

Play the game again. Try and take fewer cubes out of the pot.

sideways

up or down

diagonal

$8 \div 2$	$10 \div 5$	$9 \div 3$
$40 \div 10$	$18 \div 3$	$12 \div 4$
$12 \div 3$	$25 \div 5$	$2 \div 2$
$8 \div 4$	$12 \div 2$	$20 \div 5$
$5 \div 5$	$20 \div 4$	$3 \div 3$
$4 \div 2$	$60 \div 10$	$30 \div 5$

$30 \div 10$	$4 \div 4$
$15 \div 5$	$6 \div 2$
$24 \div 4$	$50 \div 10$
$20 \div 10$	$15 \div 3$
$10 \div 2$	$10 \div 10$
$6 \div 3$	$16 \div 4$

Now, with a friend, talk about how you could make this into a paired game.

Play the game.

If you need to, change your rules to make the best game possible.

Let's Investigate

12, 22, 42, 52, 82

Each of the numbers above has 2 left over when divided by 10.

Write 5 numbers that have 3 left over when divided by 10.

Write 5 numbers that have 7 left over when divided by 10.

Which numbers have 1 left over when divided by 5?

Which numbers have 2 left over when divided by 5?

What about numbers that have 3 or 4 left over when divided by 5?

The Puzzler

11	12	13	14	15	16

Draw lines matching a cake with a plate so that when the cake number is divided by the plate number, the answer is one of the numbers on the presents above.

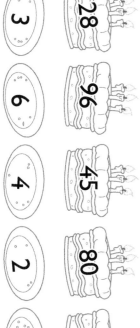

28	96	45	80	52	66
3	6	4	2	8	5

The Puzzler

Roll 2 1–6 dice and multiply the numbers together.

Look at the boxes. Write your answers on the correct box. (You can write a number on more than one box.)

If it doesn't belong anywhere, write it on the waste bin.

Roll the dice again and repeat.

If you get the same answer more than once, don't write it down.

Try and write 3 numbers on each box before you write two numbers on the waste bin.

remainder

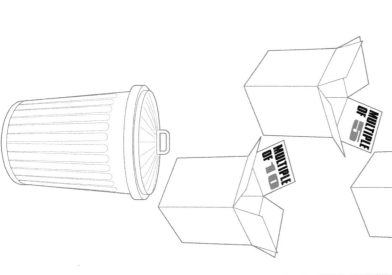

MULTIPLE OF 10

MULTIPLE OF 5

MULTIPLE OF 3

MULTIPLE OF 4

MULTIPLE OF 2

2

3

The Maths Herald

Name: _____   Date: _____

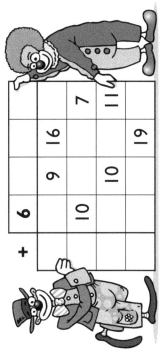

Looking for Patterns

- Think of a number.
- Add 4.
- Multiply this answer by 2.
- Subtract 6.
- Halve this answer.
- Subtract the number you first thought of.
- What's your final answer?

Repeat several times.

Start with a different number each time.

What do you notice?

- Think of a number.
- Multiply it by 5.
- Add 2.
- Double this answer.
- Subtract 4.
- Divide this answer by 10.
- What's your final answer?

Repeat several times.

Start with a different number each time.

What do you notice?

The Puzzler

Complete this addition table.

+				
6		9	16	7
	10			11
	10			19

Let's Investigate

| 1 | 2 | 3 | 4 | 5 | 6 | 7 | 8 |

| + | − | × | ÷ |

All the digits 1–8 and each of the 4 operations have been used to complete these 2 number sentences:

7 × 1 − 3 = 4

6 ÷ 2 + 5 = 8

Arrange the digits 1–8 and the 4 operations in different ways to make 2 more number sentences:

☐ ☐ ☐ ☐ = ☐

☐ ☐ ☐ ☐ = ☐

What's the Problem?

Milo visits his cousins on their farm. He counts all the chickens and goats.

Altogether he counts 10 heads and 26 legs.

How many chickens and goats are on the farm?

The Language of Maths

Write some sentences describing your class. Include in each sentence something to do with addition, subtraction, multiplication or division.

There are 28 children in our class today. 16 are having school dinners and 12 have brought packed lunches.

Let's Investigate

Look at the 3 grids below.

Complete each grid to show what happens when you add, subtract and multiply pairs of odd and even numbers.

+	ODD	EVEN
ODD	even	
EVEN		

–	ODD	EVEN
ODD		
EVEN		

×	ODD	EVEN
ODD		
EVEN		

Construct

Imagine you are an inventor.

What machine would you most like to invent?

What will your machine do?

What things would you need to make your machine?

Make a detailed drawing of your machine. Label all the parts of it.

How much does each part of your machine cost?

What is the total cost of your machine?

Money Matters

Alice and Michael have been saving their money. For every £2 that Alice saves, Michael saves £3.

- If Alice saves £8, how much does Michael save?

- If Michael saves £9, how much does Alice save?

- Together, they save a total of £30. How much have they each saved?

operator

The Maths Herald

Name:

Date:

Money Matters

Altogether 3 children have £2.50.

No 2 children have the same amount of money or the same number of coins.

What coins might each child have?

Let's Investigate

Write numbers in the boxes to complete each number sentence.

$\square + \square = 12$

$\square + \square + \square = 12$

$\square + \square + \square + \square = 12$

$\square - \square = 12$

$\square + \square = 12$

$\square \times \square = 12$

$\square \div \square = 12$

$\square \times \square = 12$

$\square - \square = 12$

Can you find more than one solution for any of the number sentences?

Let's Investigate

Using the 3 numbers in this triangle you can write 2 addition and 2 subtraction number sentences.

$3 + 4 = 7$

$4 + 3 = 7$

$7 - 4 = 3$

$7 - 3 = 4$

Draw triangles with other sets of 3 numbers that you can use to make 2 addition and 2 subtraction number sentences. Write down the number sentences.

Using the 3 numbers in this triangle you can write 2 multiplication and 2 division number sentences.

$5 \times 4 = 20$

$4 \times 5 = 20$

$20 \div 4 = 5$

$20 \div 5 = 4$

Draw triangles with other sets of 3 numbers that you can use to make 2 multiplication and 2 division number sentences. Write down the number sentences.

Money Matters

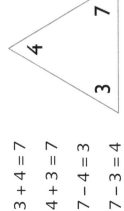

Colin has £75 in his wallet.

He has no coins, just 7 notes. The largest note is £20.

What notes does Colin have in his wallet?

The Puzzler

In each shape below, the value of the shaded section is given.

For each shape, work out the values of sections A, B and C.

Then work out the total value of each shape.

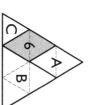

A =
B =
C =
Total =

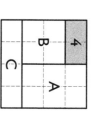

A =
B =
C =
Total =

A =
B =
C =
Total =

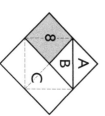

A =
B =
C =
Total =

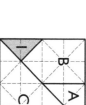

A =
B =
C =
Total =

value

The Arts Roundup

Altogether there are 28 members of the Elton Choir.

There are 6 more women in the choir than there are men.

How many men are there in the choir?

How many women are there?

Elton Choir

Let's Investigate

10 20 30 40 50 60 70 80 90 100

You can make the number 10, by adding together this pair of multiplication facts:

$(2 \times 2) + (2 \times 3)$
$= 4 + 6$
$= 10$

You can make the number 20, by adding together this pair of multiplication facts:

$(3 \times 4) + (2 \times 4)$
$= 12 + 8$
$= 20$

Make each of the other numbers above by adding together a pair of multiplication facts.

The Maths Herald

Name: Date:

Write the numbers 1–12 so that each row and column of 4 numbers totals 26.

🧩 The Puzzler

Write the numbers 1–9 so that each row and column totals the same number.

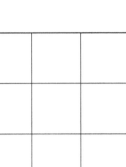

💷 Money Matters

Altogether 4 friends have a total of £20.

Fabio has £1 less than Justin.

Louise has twice as much money as Fabio.

Sarah has £4 more than Fabio.

How much money does each friend have?

🐜 What's the Problem?

Farmer Giles has some very unusual animals on his farm – emus and llamas.

How many emus and llamas does he have?

EMU   LLAMA

Altogether the emus and llamas have 28 legs and I have 1 more llama than emu.

📱 Technology Today

Play this game with a friend.

You need 1 calculator between the 2 of you.

Start with the calculator at 0.

Take turns adding 1, 2 or 3.

[+] [−] [=]   or   [+] [2] [=]   or   [+] [3] [=]

calculator

The player whose answer is 21 is the winner.

Play the game several times.

Take turns to start.

Talk about the strategies you used to help you win.

Looking for Patterns

Look at the numbers in the 2 × 2 square.

2	3
12	13

What happens when you add together pairs of numbers that are diagonally opposite each other?

2 + 13 = 15
3 + 12 = 15

Try other 2 × 2 squares. What about pairs of diagonally opposite numbers in a 3 × 3 square?

31	32	33
41	42	43
51	52	53

Investigate pairs of diagonally opposite numbers in 4 × 4 squares and 5 × 5 squares. What do you find?

1	2	3	4	5	6	7	8	9	10
11	12	13	14	15	16	17	18	19	20
21	22	23	24	25	26	27	28	29	30
31	32	33	34	35	36	37	38	39	40
41	42	43	44	45	46	47	48	49	50
51	52	53	54	55	56	57	58	59	60
61	62	63	64	65	66	67	68	69	70
71	72	73	74	75	76	77	78	79	80
81	82	83	84	85	86	87	88	89	90
91	92	93	94	95	96	97	98	99	100

 What's the Problem?

Miss Walker's class are trying to find out how old she is. But Miss Walker really doesn't want to tell them. Instead she tells them this problem. How old is Miss Walker?

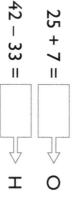

> I am more than 20, but less than 30.
> If you divide my age by 2 you are left with 1.
> If you divide my age by 3 you are left with 2.
> If you divide my age by 5 you are left with 4.

 The Language of Maths

The numbers on the right are a message written in code.

To read the message you first have to work out the answer to each number sentence and then use the letter beside it.

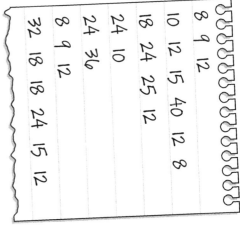

8 9 12
10 12 15 40 12 8
18 24 25 12
24 10
24 36
8 9 12
32 18 18 24 15 12

25 + 7 = [ ] → O

42 − 33 = [ ] → H

80 ÷ 2 = [ ] → R

24 ÷ 2 = [ ] → E

8 × 3 = [ ] → I

35 − 17 = [ ] → T

2 × 5 = [ ] → S

100 ÷ 4 = [ ] → L

15 + 21 = [ ] → N

5 × 3 = [ ] → C

21 ÷ 3 = [ ] → B

15 − 7 = [ ] → F

Use the code to make your own secret message, or why not invent your own spy code?

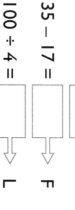

S&C Volume 2

The Maths Herald

Name:

Date:

Money Matters

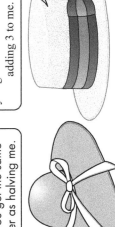

Apples cost 40p each and oranges cost 30p each.

Sally bought twice as many oranges as apples.

Altogether she spent £3.

How many apples did Sally buy?

How many oranges?

The Puzzler

What numbers are under the hats?

If you add 18 to me, you get the same answer as multiplying me by 10.

If you subtract 6 from me, you get the same answer as halving me.

If you multiply me by 4, you get the same answer as adding 3 to me.

Technology Today

Beth invited her 2 friends, James and Sam, on a picnic.

James and Sam each invited 3 friends on the picnic.

Altogether how many friends went for a picnic?

Write about how you worked out the answer.

MESSAGE
Fancy a picnic?
Tonight @ 7.
Green Park.
Bring food.

estimation

Money Matters

At Nico's *Take-and-Eat*, a burger and a kebab cost £9 altogether.

A kebab and a pie cost £7 altogether.

How much does a burger cost?

What is the cost of a kebab?

PRICES
Burger ....
Pie ....
Fish £3
Chips ....
Drinks ....

Let's Investigate

- Choose a number less than 20.
- If the number is even, halve the number.
- If the number is odd, add 3.
- Repeat until you get to 1 or the pattern starts to repeat itself.

Example 1

7
7 + 3 = 10
10 ÷ 2 = 5
5 + 3 = 8
8 ÷ 2 = 4
4 ÷ 2 = 2
2 ÷ 2 = 1

Starting with the number 7, the pattern has 6 steps and ends in 1.

Example 2

15
15 + 3 = 18
18 ÷ 2 = 9
9 + 3 = 12
12 ÷ 2 = 6
6 ÷ 2 = 3
3 + 3 = 6

Starting with the number 15, the pattern starts to repeat itself after 5 steps.

Try different starting numbers less than 20.
How many steps do different starting numbers have?
What starting numbers end in 1?
What starting numbers repeat themselves?
What patterns do you notice?

Looking for Patterns

The numbers on the balls are all approximations for the 6 number sentences.

Draw lines matching each number sentence to a 'sensible' approximation.

Then work out the answer to each number sentence and see if your approximations were right.

23 + 14 + 16

28 + 58   70

86 − 47   90   40

12 × 6   50

58 ÷ 2   20

63 ÷ 3   30

What's the Problem?

There are 30 children in Mrs Rose's Year 3 class.

All the children sit at tables of 5.

On each table there are 3 girls and 2 boys.

How many girls are there in Mrs Rose's class?

How many boys are there?

Write about how you worked out the answers.

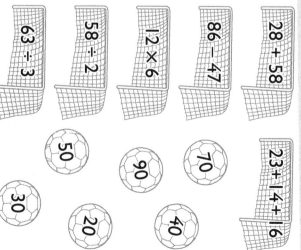

The Maths Herald

Name:

Date:

Number sentences

5	+	7	=	12
6	×	5	=	30
16	÷	2	=	8
15	–	4	=	11

inverse operation

The Puzzler

On the sheet, write 4 different number sentences like those on the right.

You can use addition, subtraction, multiplication and division.

Write each number and each symbol on a separate card.

Then cut out the 20 cards and shuffle them.

Give your set of cards to a friend and see if they can make your 4 number sentences.

Keep a copy so you can remember what you wrote!

Technology Today

Look at the mobile phone.

1	2	3
4	5	6
7	8	9
*	0	#

Add all the digits in the **left column**.

Add all the digits in the **middle column**.

Add all the digits in the **right column**.

Add all the digits in the **first row**.

Add all the digits in the **second row**.

Add all the digits in the **third row**.

Add all the digits in this diagonal.

Add all the digits in this diagonal.

What patterns do you notice?

The Puzzler

A multiplication sign is missing from the circle in this number sentence.

4 ◯ 10 = 40

A division sign is missing from the circle in this number sentence.

10 ◯ 2 = 5

Write the × or ÷ sign that is missing from each circle in these number sentences.

80 ◯ 8 = 10

9 ◯ 5 = 45

42 ◯ 6 = 7

33 ◯ 3 = 11

400 ◯ 4 = 100

45 ◯ 9 = 5

7 ◯ 10 = 70

100 ◯ 5 = 20

Let's Investigate

Using no more than 3 darts for each number, can you make all the numbers from 1 to 30?

If a dart hits the inner grey ring the score is double (× 2) the amount of the outer ring.

Here are 2 to get you started.

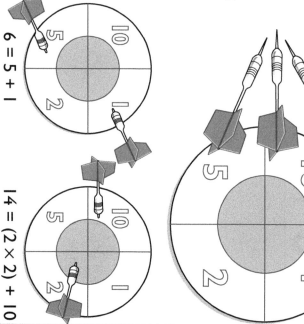

$6 = 5 + 1$

$14 = (2 \times 2) + 10$

Technology Today

Every time Habiba spends £10 on mobile phone calls she gets 50 free texts.

Habiba has had 250 free texts.

How much money has Habiba spent on mobile phone calls?

If Habiba spends £80 on mobile phone calls how many free texts does she get?

How did you work out the answers?

Money Matters

Leroy pays for 1 banana with the exact amount of money.

How many different ways could Leroy have paid for the banana?

Here is 1 way:

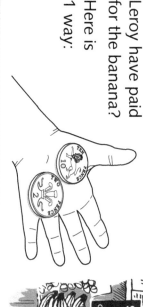

SPECIAL
Bananas
only 12p each

Let's Investigate

Use 6 counters to make a path from 1 to STOP.

What is the total of the 6 numbers?

How many different totals can you make?

 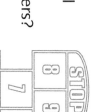

Rearrange the digits 1–9 to make the largest possible total.

Rearrange the digits 1–9 to make the smallest possible total.

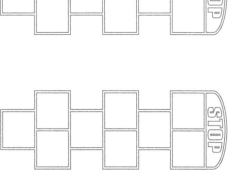 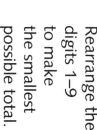

The Maths Herald

S&C Volume 2

Name:

Date:

Construct

Leo's mum always cuts his sandwiches into equal pieces.

Using square pieces of paper show what Leo's sandwiches might look like.

Let's Investigate

What things are just as good (or half as good!) if they are cut in half?

Make a list.

What things are ruined if they are cut in half?

Make another list.

Let's Investigate

The fraction wall here shows halves and quarters of 40 km.

40 km	
20 km	20 km
10 km	10 km	10 km	10 km

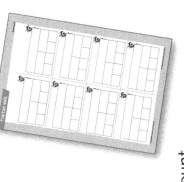

Use the fraction walls on the sheet to show halves and quarters of these different amounts:

20p   £1

32 litres   1 kg

1 day   1 dozen eggs

For the last 2 fraction walls on the sheet, write 2 different amounts of your own and find halves and quarters of each amount.

Let's Investigate

Work with a friend.

Place 12 blue and 12 yellow cubes into a bag or a box.

Take turns to take out 8 cubes.

dozen

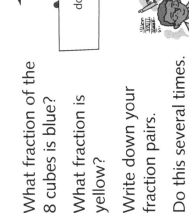

What fraction of the 8 cubes is blue?

What fraction is yellow?

Write down your fraction pairs.

Do this several times.

Now choose 10 or 12 cubes.

Say how many of each colour you have.

Let's Investigate

Look at the 2 large squares.

Half of each square has been shaded to make a pattern.

Make other patterns by shading half a large square.

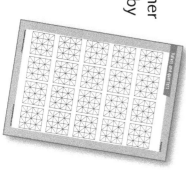

What's the Problem?

Take a lump of modelling clay.

How can you divide the clay exactly in half?

Now divide it into quarters.

How can you check that your modelling clay has been divided exactly in halves and quarters?

Write about what you did.

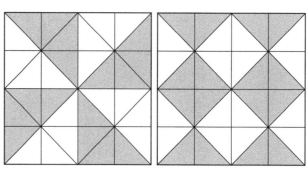

Looking for Patterns

You have a box of white tiles and a box of blue tiles.

They can be cut in halves or quarters in these four different ways.

The pieces can then be arranged to make different patterned tiles like these.

What other patterned tiles can you make using white and blue pieces?

Draw your patterned tiles on squared paper.

Looking for Patterns

Find the rule and write the next 3 numbers.

$\frac{1}{4}$	$\frac{2}{4}$	$\frac{3}{4}$	1	$1\frac{1}{4}$	
$\frac{1}{3}$	$\frac{2}{3}$	1	$1\frac{1}{3}$	$1\frac{2}{3}$	
2	$2\frac{1}{2}$	3	$3\frac{1}{2}$	4	
$\frac{1}{4}$	$\frac{1}{2}$	$\frac{3}{4}$	1	$1\frac{1}{4}$	

What do you notice about the first and last number lines?

S&C Volume 2

The Maths Herald

Name:

Date:

The Language of Maths

When do you use fractions to describe something? Make a list.

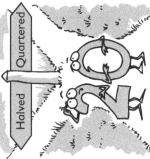

You can have half.

share equally

Let's Investigate

Write 4 lists:

- Numbers that can be halved equally.
- Numbers that cannot be halved equally.
- Numbers that can be shared into quarters equally.
- Numbers that cannot be shared into quarters equally.

Write numbers between 1 and 100 on your lists.

Can you find some numbers that belong on more than one list?

Can you write any larger numbers on your lists?

Halved | Quartered

Let's Investigate

Look at the 2 large squares.

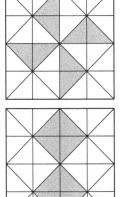

One-quarter of each square has been shaded to make a pattern.

What other patterns can you make by shading one-quarter of a large square?

Draw your patterns on the sheet.

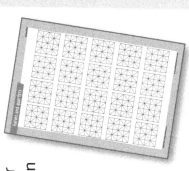

At Home

This weekend keep a record of what fraction of the sky is covered by cloud.

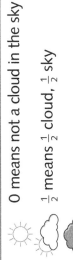
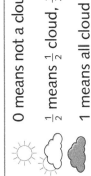

- 0 means not a cloud in the sky
- $\frac{1}{2}$ means $\frac{1}{2}$ cloud, $\frac{1}{2}$ sky
- 1 means all cloud

Do this 3 times each day – morning, afternoon and evening.

Use this table to record your findings.

Place a tick ✓ in the most suitable box.

	Saturday			Sunday		
	Morning	Afternoon	Evening	Morning	Afternoon	Evening
0						
$\frac{1}{4}$						
$\frac{1}{2}$						
$\frac{3}{4}$						
1						

The Puzzler

Hayley and Aimee are twins.

On their birthday they each had a birthday cake.

Hayley cut her birthday cake into 8 equal pieces with 4 straight cuts.

Draw what Hayley did.

HAPPY BIRTHDAY HAYLEY

Aimee cut her birthday cake into 9 equal pieces with 4 straight cuts.

Draw what Aimee did.

HAPPY BIRTHDAY AIMEE

Let's Investigate

Look at the sheet. It shows lots of large rectangles divided into eighths.

How many different ways can you do this?

What do you notice about the number of red and blue rectangles you have shaded in each large rectangle?

On each rectangle, shade:
- $\frac{1}{8}$ yellow
- $\frac{1}{4}$ red
- $\frac{2}{8}$ blue
- $\frac{3}{8}$ green.

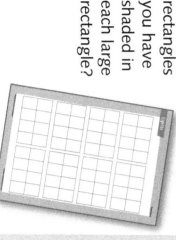

Construct

Bruno cuts a pizza into equal pieces.

Using circular pieces of paper, show what his pizza might look like.

Let's Investigate

Look at some different fruits that can be easily divided into segments. Tangerines and satsumas are great for this, so too are oranges.

Peel each fruit and take the segments apart.

How many segments does each fruit have?

What fraction of the whole fruit is 1 segment?

What fraction of the whole fruit are 2, 3, 4 … segments?

Does the same fruit always have the same number of segments?

Draw or write about your findings.

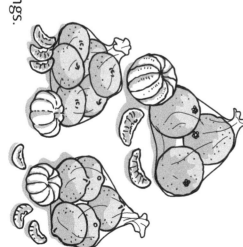

S&C Volume 2

The Maths Herald

Name:

Date:

🐭 The Puzzler

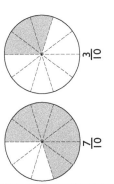

- How many faces have hair? What fraction is this?
- How many faces are sad and wearing a hat? What fraction is this?
- How many faces have hair and are wearing glasses? What fraction is this?
- How many faces have a round face? What fraction is this?
- How many faces have their eyes open? What fraction is this?
- How many faces are happy? What fraction is this?

🐜 Let's Investigate

Ask a friend to measure how tall you are. Write this down.

Now find something in the classroom that is about $\frac{1}{2}$ as long or as tall as your height. What is it, and what is its measurement?

Can you find something that is about $\frac{1}{4}$ of your height?

What about $\frac{1}{5}$ or $\frac{1}{3}$ of your height?

🐜 Let's Investigate

These 2 fractions make a whole.

$\frac{7}{10}$ $\frac{3}{10}$

What other pairs of fractions make a whole?

Can you find groups of 3 fractions that make a whole?

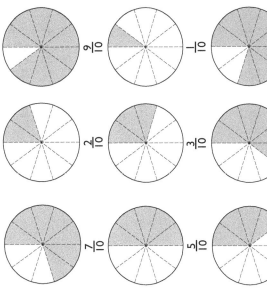

$\frac{9}{10}$ $\frac{2}{10}$ $\frac{7}{10}$

$\frac{1}{10}$ $\frac{3}{10}$ $\frac{5}{10}$

$\frac{8}{10}$ $\frac{6}{10}$ $\frac{4}{10}$

Sports Update

Mrs Wilson is in charge of looking after the PE cupboard.

How many tennis balls are there in the PE cupboard?

How many balls are there altogether?

Write about how you worked out the answers.

Half of all the balls are tennis balls. There are also 7 footballs, 3 softballs and 2 basketballs.

What's the Problem?

On Monday Jamal bought a packet of 64 chocolate drops and ate half the pack.

On Tuesday he ate half of what was left.

On Wednesday he ate half of what was left.

Jamal did the same thing each day until there was only one chocolate drop left.

On which day was this?

Write about how you worked out the answer.

one tenth

Money Matters

Mrs Thomas has decided that she will spend a total of £120 on her 4 grandchildren for their birthdays this year.

She says how she has decided to share out the money.

How much money will Mrs Thomas spend on each of her grandchildren?

Show all your working.

I will spend half of the money on Tom. I will spend a quarter of the money on Lisa. Whatever is left, I will spend half on Sam and half on Lee.

The Arts Roundup

Roxy Theatre is putting on the show 'Music in Springtime'.

On Tuesday there were 40 people watching the show and the theatre was $\frac{1}{3}$ full.

The seating plan shows which seats were occupied.

On Wednesday the theatre is only $\frac{1}{4}$ full.

How many people watch the show on Wednesday?

Write about how you worked out the answer.

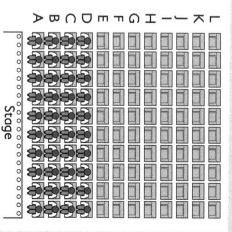

Stage

© HarperCollinsPublishers 2016

The Maths Herald

Name:

Date:

In the Past

Imagine a time before rulers, metre sticks and tape measures.

How might you measure each of the following:

- the length of a field?
- the width of a river?
- the height of a tree?

What would be the advantages and disadvantages of using your system?

Focus on Science

The heights of 5 trees are 12 metres, 9 metres, $7\frac{1}{2}$ metres, 6 metres and 6 metres.

The yew is the same height as the pine, but shorter than the beech.

The beech is shorter than the poplar but taller than the elm.

How tall is each tree?

Sports Update

- How far are 3 laps of the track?
- How many laps of the track is 1 km?

1 lap = 200 m

In a 4 × 100 m relay race, 4 runners each run 100 m.

- What fraction of the track does each runner run?
- What is the total distance of the race?
- How many laps of the track is this?

In a 4 × 400 m relay race, 4 runners each run 400 m.

- How many laps of the track does each runner run?
- What is the total distance of the race?
- How many laps of the track is this?

Let's Investigate

Estimate how many interlocking cubes you would need to build a wall 2 metres long and 1 cube high.

Write about how you made your estimate.

Now use interlocking cubes to find out how close your estimate was.

How tall a wall do you think you can build from interlocking cubes before it starts wobbling and falls down? Build a wall to see how close your estimate was.

Focus on Science

What is the height of the tallest tree in your school playground? How might you go about finding out? Try this method.

- Place a stick in the ground and measure its height.

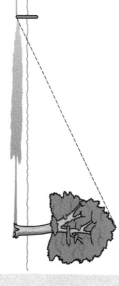

- Measure the length of the shadow of the stick.
- Measure the length of the shadow of the tree.
- Multiply the height of the stick by the length of the tree's shadow.
- Divide the answer by the length of the stick's shadow.

This is the height of the tree! What other things could you find the height of using this method? What about the height of the tallest person in school?

Sports Update

Approximately how many skipping ropes are there in your school?

There are probably 2 different types of skipping ropes. Short ones to use by yourself and long ones to use with a group.

Estimate the total length of all the skipping ropes in your school. Write about how you made your estimate.

2

In the Past

Here is another method of finding out the height of the tallest tree in your school playground. It was used by Native Americans for many years.

- Stand with your back to the tree.
- Walk away from the tree.
- Stop when you can look between your legs and just see the top of the tree.

distance

- Measure how far you are from the base of the tree.

This is the same as the height of the tree! What other things could you find the height of using this method?

What about the height of the tallest person in school? Compare this method with the method in the Focus on Science activity on page 2.

The Language of Maths

length

Make a list of words to do with length.

3

The Maths Herald

Name:

Date:

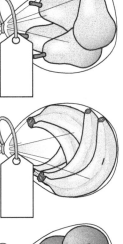

What's the Problem?

Sylvia buys 4 bags of fruit.

Each bag of fruit weighs a different amount: 1 kg, $1\frac{1}{2}$ kg, 2 kg and 3 kg.

The apples weigh more than the pears.

The pears weigh less than the oranges.

The bananas weigh more than the oranges.

The bananas weigh less than the apples.

Write the weight on each bag of fruit.

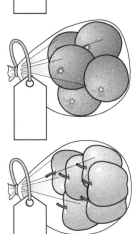

Focus on Science

In what ways are you smaller than a baby elephant?

In what ways are you larger than a baby elephant?

The Language of Maths

mass

Make a list of words to do with mass.

Let's Investigate

A game to play with a friend.

Use items from one of the containers, for example, the interlocking cubes.

Take turns to roll the dice and collect that many cubes.

Put the cubes on the balance or scales.

Keep playing until the cubes weigh more than 500 g.

Play the game several times using a different container of items each game.

Which game took the longest to play? Which game was quickest? Why?

You need:

- balance and a 500 g ($\frac{1}{2}$ kg) weight or a set of kitchen scales
- container of interlocking cubes
- container of pennies
- container of marbles
- container of counters
- 0 – 9 dice

mass

At Home

Find 10 different types of packaged food in the kitchen cupboard.

Without looking at any labels, write the names of these 10 items in order, starting with the lightest.

If some of the contents have already been used, estimate the mass when full.

When you have finished your list, look at the labels on each of the items.

Write another list ordering the mass of each item, starting with the lightest.

Compare your 2 lists.

At Home

Next time you visit a supermarket, go to the fruit and vegetable section.

With the help of an adult, look at the labels.

For each fruit and vegetable write down the mass.

The mass might be for 1 item or for a pack.

If the mass is for a pack, estimate how many items there are in a pack. Write this down also. Ask whoever is with you to tell you the approximate mass of 1 item.

Make a long list of different fruits and vegetables.

When you get home, order your list of fruit and vegetables, from lightest to heaviest.

2

The Puzzler

You only have these weights:

Balance each scale by drawing on the missing weights.

Let's Investigate

You will need a set of kitchen scales and a set of bathroom scales for this activity.

Choose an object in the classroom. Use the kitchen scales to weigh it.

Write down the mass of the object.

Use the bathroom scales to weigh yourself.

Write down your mass. Now hold the object you chose. Weigh yourself again on the bathroom scales. Write down the total mass.

What do you notice?

Choose different objects, some heavy and some light, and repeat the activity several times.

What do you notice?

The Maths Herald

Name: Date:

Focus on Science

Take a large, clear, plastic measuring jug half full of water.

Find a collection of objects that will each fit in the jug and not be spoilt if they get wet.

Place one of the objects in the jug.

What happens to the level of the water?

Take this object out and repeat for each of the other objects.

For each object write about what happens to the level of the water.

Write some sentences explaining your results.

displacement

The Language of Maths

What is volume?
What is capacity?

Construct

Use interlocking cubes to build a box that will hold exactly 20 pencils.

Use some other construction material to build another box to hold exactly 20 pencils.

Use another type of construction material to build a third box to hold exactly 20 pencils.

Which box is best? Why?

Focus on Science

Who do you think has the largest fist?

Take a large, clear, plastic measuring jug half full of water.

Make sure that the jug is exactly half full of water.

Read the scale on the jug. How much water is in the jug?

Find a friend. Ask them to make a fist and put it into the jug of water.

Tell them to hold their hand steady while you read the scale on the jug.

Write down what it reads.

Repeat for 5 other friends.

Write about your results. What conclusions can you make?

Let's Investigate

Copy this table.

Capacity	Container
Less than $\frac{1}{2}$ l	
Between $\frac{1}{2}$ l and 1 l	
Exactly 1 l	
Between 1 l and 2 l	
More than 2 l	

Look around your classroom for different containers.

Look at the labels on these containers. List each container on the table.

If there are any containers without labels, try and estimate their capacities.

At Home

Approximately how much water do you waste if you leave the tap running while you brush your teeth?

You will need to think carefully about how you are going to measure this!

How much water is wasted in a week?

How much is this in a month?

What about in a year?

Let's Investigate

For this activity you will need the help of the school caretaker.

A water meter is an instrument that measures how much water is used.

Ask the caretaker to show you the school's water meter.

There will be a number on the water metre. Write down the number.

Ask the caretaker to tell you what this number means.

Every day for a week, check the water meter and write down the number shown.

Write about what has happened. Why do you think this is?

You may have a water meter at home. Find out about how much water you use at home in a week!

Let's Investigate

Take 1 container at a time and estimate where you think 1 cupful of water will come to. If you can, make this mark on the container.

When you have done this for each container, check your estimates. Write about your results.

You need:
- a cup
- lots of different containers larger than the cup such as jugs, bottles, yoghurt pots
- some water
- a funnel

S&C Volume 2

The Maths Herald

Name:

Date:

Happy Birthday Patricia, Janet, Leo and Stanley

calendar

What's the Problem?

Leo, Stanley, Patricia and Janet all celebrate their birthday on the same day.

Leo is 4 years younger than Patricia.

Janet is half the age of Patricia.

Next year Patricia will be 13 years old.

Stanley is twice as old as Leo.

How old is each person?

I'm allowed to watch 2 hours of television a night.

I'm allowed to watch 3 television programmes a night.

Let's Investigate

Who do you think watches more TV each week? Why?

Use a TV guide to plan a week's TV viewing for both Jamie and Natalie.

Who watches more TV each week?

Construct

Work with a friend to build a 1 minute sand timer.

Think about:

- what things you are going to need
- how you are going to go about building it.

Try and make your timer as close to 1 minute as possible.

When you have finished, write about what you did.

Construct

Design a calendar for your class for the next half of the term.

Find out from your teacher the start and finish dates for the next half of the term.

Your calendar needs to show the months of the year, the dates in the month and the days of the week.

Draw a rough classroom calendar to start with.

When you've designed the perfect calendar for your class, make a larger one that can go on display. Use it to record important events for your class for the next half term.

The Arts Roundup

The Meroo Opera Theatre puts on lots of different shows during the year.

Complete their calendar below.

The Meroo Opera Theatre
Diary of Events

January 2 – January 17 ———— Christmas Pantomime
January 23 – February 28 ———— Berry Opera Company
March 6 – March 28 — Hills Dramatic Society
April 10 – May 2 — Valley Symphony Orchestra
May 15 – June 27 — Wilton Ballet Company
July 3 – July 24 — Alps Youth Orchestra
September 11 – October 10 — Valley Big Brass Band
October 23 – November 28 — Orange Theatre Company
December 11 – December 23 — Christmas Pantomime

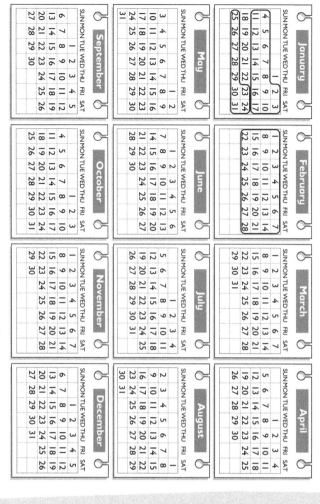

How many days in the year is there a performance in the theatre?

How many days is there no performance in the theatre?

The Language of Maths

time

Make a list of words to do with time.

What's the Problem?

In spring, Steve the gardener is very busy.

Every 3rd day he has to water the flowers.

Every 4th day he has to weed the garden.

Every 5th day he has to cut the grass.

On April 3rd, Steve had a very long day. He had to water the flowers, weed the garden and cut the grass.

When will Steve next have to water the flowers, weed the garden and cut the grass all on the same day?

Use the calendars to help you.

X water flowers
O weed garden
☐ cut grass

The Maths Herald

Name:

Date:

Let's Investigate

What is the furthest (maximum) distance that you and a friend can stand apart to throw and catch a ball?

First make an estimate.

Carry out an experiment to find the maximum distance.

Write about your results and what you did.

What's the Problem?

At *Ted's Hardware* you can buy wood and Ted will cut it to whatever lengths you want.

Ted has an order to cut a 4 metre piece of wood into 8 equal lengths.

It takes Ted 2 minutes to make each cut.

- How many minutes will it take him to cut all 8 lengths?
- How long is each length of wood?

Ted's Hardware

Focus on Science

Is this true?

What if you use different sizes of paper?

Write about your results.

It's impossible to fold a sheet of paper in half more than 7 times.

Use sheets of paper from the recycling bin.

Focus on Science

Temperature is the measurement we use to describe how hot or cold something is.

Each day, newspapers give the lowest (called 'minimum') and highest (called 'maximum') temperatures.

Look through a newspaper and find the nearest place to where you live that gives the temperature.

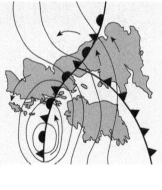

Record your results in the table.

Do this for each day of the week.

At the end of the week, write about the temperature during the week.

	lowest (minimum) temperature	highest (maximum) temperature
Monday		
Tuesday		
Wednesday		
Thursday		
Friday		

Focus on Science

List as many different measuring tools as you can think of.

Briefly describe what each tool is used to measure.

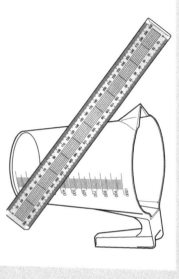

The Language of Maths

Derek likes to exaggerate when he talks.

Look at these statements that Derek has said.

> I walk 10 miles to school each morning.

> I can lift up something that weighs 250 kilograms.

> When we flew from London to Sydney, it only took us 5 hours.

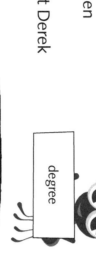

degree

> Yesterday I drank 100 litres of water.

Rewrite each of these statements so that they are believable.

Around the World

How far do you travel to and from school each day?

Who in your class travels the furthest distance? How far is this?

Who travels the shortest distance? How far is this?

At Home

Find some eggs.

Choose an egg and call it Egg 1.

Measure the width around the middle of the egg. Be careful not to break it!

Record your results for Egg 1.

Do the same for some other eggs, calling them Egg 2, Egg 3, Egg 4, and so on, recording your results.

Measure the distance around the egg from top to bottom and back.

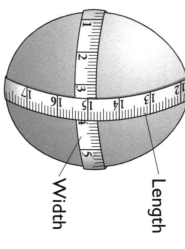

Length

Width

Are all the eggs the same size?

If not, write down the order of your eggs, smallest to largest.

Can you work out the weight of each of your eggs? If so, record your results.

The Maths Herald

Name:

Date:

Sports Update

Every week Tamsin runs 1 km more than the week before.

If she ran 2 km for the first week and this week she is running 12 km, for how many weeks has Tamsin been running?

The Puzzler

How many kilograms does each bag weigh?

Bags of the same type weigh the same.

HINT

The lightest bag weighs 2 kg.

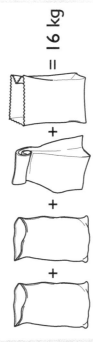 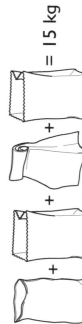 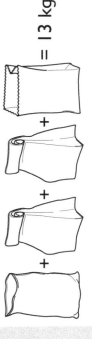

+ + + = 16 kg

+ + + = 15 kg

+ + + = 13 kg

The Language of Maths

Look through a selection of newspapers and magazines.

Find as many different examples of measuring words such as more, less, the biggest, the longest, and so on.

Cut out the words and make them into a poster.

Beside each word write what is being measured.

What's the Problem?

The moon is shining at midnight.

Will it be daylight in 72 hours time?

How did you work out the answer?

Around the World

What jobs use measuring tools?

Write a list of as many different jobs as you can think of.

What types of measuring tools does each job use?

Sort these jobs into different groups.

Can you sort them in different ways?

Focus on Science

Temperature is the measurement we use to describe how hot or cold something is.

Just as there are different units to measure distance: kilometre and mile, so too there are different units we can use to measure temperature.

These are called degrees Fahrenheit (°F) or degrees Celsius (°C).

We measure temperature using a thermometer.

The thermometers below show the temperature in 6 different cities.

What is the temperature in each city?

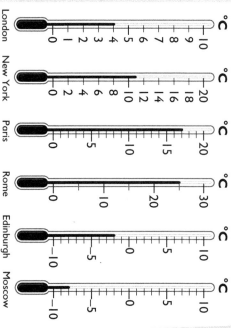

London   New York   Paris   Rome   Edinburgh   Moscow

The Language of Maths

Look at the temperature readings for Edinburgh and Moscow in the Focus on Science activity on page 2.

What do these temperatures mean?

Focus on Science

Use a thermometer to investigate each of the following:

• How the temperature in your classroom changes during one day.

• How the temperature in your classroom changes during one week.

• How the temperature in your classroom is different from 2 other places in your school.

Think about how best to display your results.

You might use a table or a graph.

Write about what you did.

Write about your results.

scale

The Maths Herald

Name:

Date:

The Puzzler

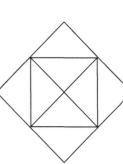

vertex

The diagram on the right shows 6 small squares.

Make this shape using 17 matchsticks.

How can you:

- remove 2 matches to make 5 small squares?
- remove 4 matches to make 4 small squares?
- remove 5 matches to make 4 small squares?
- remove 3 matches to make 4 small squares?
- remove 4 matches to make 3 squares?
- Draw your results on squared dot paper.

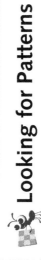

Looking for Patterns

How many squares can you see?

Construct

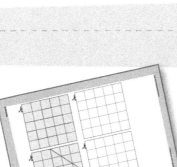

Cut out the 1st shape on the sheet.

Jumble up the 5 pieces then try and put the shape back together again.

Do the same with the 2nd shape.

Now that you have completed the 2 square shape jigsaw puzzles, make 2 square shape jigsaw puzzles of your own for a friend to solve.

RULES:

- Each jigsaw must have exactly 5 pieces.
- You can only make pieces using the grid lines or by drawing lines diagonally through a square like this ◹ or like this ◺.

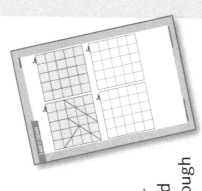

Let's Investigate

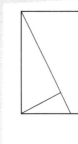

Cut out the 1st shape.

Can you arrange the 2 pieces to make shapes with 3, 4, 5, 6 and 7 sides?

Draw your results.

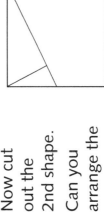

Now cut out the 2nd shape.

Can you arrange the 3 pieces to make shapes with 3, 4, 5, 6, 7 and 8 sides?

Draw your results.

Let's Investigate

Use 4 squares from the sheet to make different shapes.

Note: These 2 shapes are the same.

Draw your different shapes on squared paper.

What if you used 5 squares?

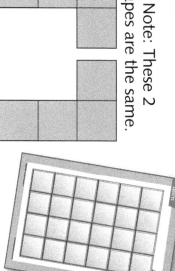

Looking for Patterns

1 triangle and 1 square have a total of 7 sides.

1 triangle and 1 pentagon have a total of 8 sides.

Two squares also have a total of 8 sides.

What shapes have a total of 9 sides?

What about 10 / 11 / 12 / 13 sides?

Let's Investigate

You can make these squares on a 2 × 2 square geoboard.

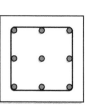
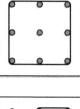
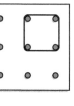
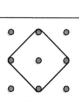

How many different sized squares can you draw on a 3 × 3 square geoboard?

What about on a 4 × 4 square geoboard?

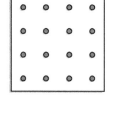

Draw your results on squared dot paper.

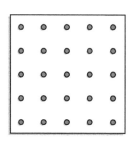

Construct

Look at the 5 shapes below. Only the corners of each shape are shown.

Name each of the shapes.

Can you draw shapes for a hexagon and an octagon in the same way?

The Maths Herald

Name:

Date:

Sports Update

Find a football.

Is a football a perfect sphere?

What 2-D shapes are used to make up a football?

How many of each of these shapes are there?

Construct

Look at the 4 drawings below. Only the corners of each 3-D shape are shown.

Name each of the shapes.

Can you draw a similar diagram for a cuboid?

3-D

The Language of Maths

cube   cuboid   sphere   cylinder   cone
squared-based pyramid   triangular-based pyramid

Write a description for each of these shapes on a separate piece of paper.

Do not write the name of the shape on the piece of paper.

You must be able to tell from your descriptions exactly what each shape is.

Give your descriptions to a friend.

Can they name each shape from your descriptions?

I think that this is a sphere.

At Home

What objects can you find at home that are battery-powered?

Make a list of all these objects.

Include the following:

- the number of batteries the object uses
- the name or type of battery
- the shape of the battery.

Here is an example:

My computer mouse uses 2 AA batteries.

The batteries are cylinders.

4

Sports Update

Go to the school playground.

What equipment can you see that is made using 3-D shapes?

Make a list of all the 3-D shapes you can see.

What 3-D shapes can you find in the sports cupboard?

If your school has a nursery play area, what 3-D shapes can you see there?

Construct

Design your own junk model robot.

Draw a sketch of your robot.

Think about the different shapes you need to build your robot and the types of junk that you could use.

Label your sketch of the robot showing the pieces of junk you would use.

Construct

Each of these models is made using interlocking cubes.

How many cubes were needed to build each model?

Now use interlocking cubes to build a model of your own.

Look carefully at your model. Find a view where you cannot count the total number of cubes.

Ask a friend to view your model from this position. Can they say how many cubes were needed to build your model?

What do you notice about your answers?

The Language of Maths

Look at the model you made in the ⚡ Construct activity above.

Imagine you had to explain your model to someone over the telephone.

Write a set of instructions telling them how to make it.

Now give your instructions to a friend. (Don't show them your model.)

Can they copy your model?

The Maths Herald

Name:

Date:

Let's Investigate

Look at the 6 large squares at the top of the sheet.

Here is one to get you started.

Now look at the 6 large squares at the bottom of the sheet.

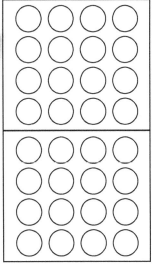

On the 1st square use 1 colour to shade half the triangles to make a symmetrical pattern.

Draw in the line of symmetry.

Make a different symmetrical pattern in each of the other large squares.

Here is one to get you started.

On the 1st square use 1 colour to shade half the squares to make a symmetrical pattern.

Draw in the line of symmetry.

Make a different symmetrical pattern in each of the other large squares.

Let's Investigate

Look at the 7 patterns of circles on the sheet.

Using only 1 colour, make a different symmetrical pattern in each of the 7 rectangles.

Here is one to get you started.

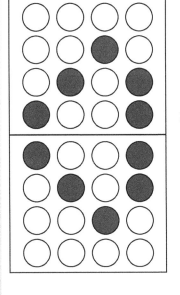

Let's Investigate

Look at the 7 patterns of circles on the sheet.

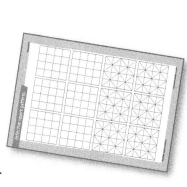

On the 1st pattern, use only 1 colour to make a symmetrical pattern by colouring 6 circles only.

On the 2nd pattern, use only 1 colour to make a symmetrical pattern by colouring 8 circles only.

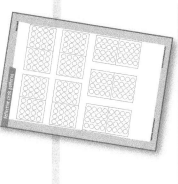

Continue for the other 5 patterns, colouring 10, 12, 14, 16 and 18 circles.

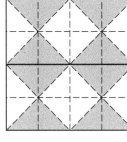

line of symmetry

The Language of Maths

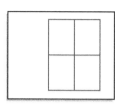

Draw a large 2 × 2 grid on a sheet of paper.

Write your first name in the

First box.

Reflect your name in the other 3 boxes.

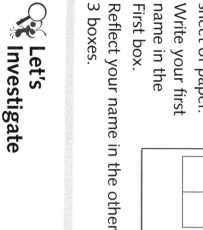

When you have finished, turn your sheet of paper upside down.

What do you notice?

	First Write your name here	
	mirror	
Third Reflect your name here	mirror	Second Reflect your name here
	mirror	
	Last Reflect your name here	

Let's Investigate

Look at the 6 large squares at the top of the sheet.

Using 4 colours make a different symmetrical pattern in each of the six squares.

Draw in the line of symmetry on each square.

Here is 1 to get you started.

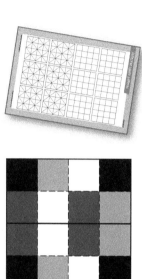

Now look at the 6 large squares at the bottom of the sheet.

Using 4 colours make a different symmetrical pattern in each of the 6 squares. Draw in the line of symmetry on each square.

Here is one to get you started.

The Language of Maths

A B C D E F G H I J K L M N O P Q R S T U V W X Y Z

Look at the letters above. Which letters have symmetry?

Do they show vertical symmetry or horizontal symmetry?

vertical symmetry   horizontal symmetry

A   B

What about these lower case letters?

a b c d e f g h i j k l m n o p q r s t u v w x y z

The Puzzler

Look at these words.

Place a mirror on the lines then draw the reflection to complete each word.

CHECK   BOOK

BIKE   MAT

Now choose a word and write it in the same way.

Only choose letters that you discovered in The Language of Maths activity above that show symmetry.

Give your word to a friend to complete.

The Maths Herald

Name:

Date:

coordinates

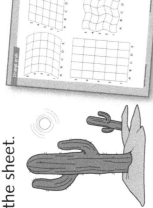

The Puzzler

Read the clues to colour the stars and solve the puzzle.

You need red, green, blue, yellow, black and purple coloured pencils.

Clue 1: There are 3 green stars and they are all in the top row, but they do not touch each other.

Clue 2: There is a red star above the blue star.

Clue 3: The purple star has a green star to its left and to its right.

Clue 4: The black star is below the purple star.

Clue 5: 2 of the red stars are below green stars.

Clue 6: The yellow star is in the bottom left corner next to the blue star.

Construct

Copy the picture 4 times using the different grids on the sheet.

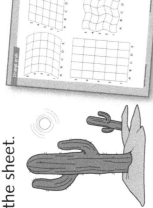

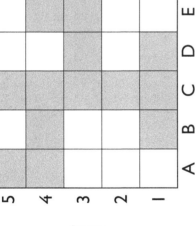

	A	B	C	D	E
5					
4					
3					
2					
1					

Around the World

Find a map of the world.

Put a small counter over the place that is nearest to where you live.

Find 5 countries or cities that are:

- north (N) of where you live
- south (S) of where you live
- east (E) of where you live
- west (W) of where you live.

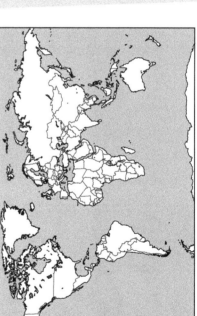

The Language of Maths

Look at the first grid. It shows a route through the squares from Start to Finish. Underneath the route are the directions.

Write the directions for the second grid.

For the third grid, follow the directions and draw the route.

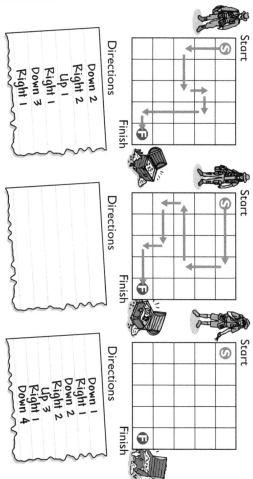

Grid 1 — Directions
Down 2
Right 2
Up 1
Right 1
Down 3
Right 1

Grid 2 — Directions
(blank)

Grid 3 — Directions
Down 1
Right 1
Down 2
Right 2
Up 3
Right 1
Down 4

Now, using squared paper, draw a route from a starting point to a finishing point.

Rules:
- You can only move left or right and up or down.
- Diagonals are not allowed.
- You can only move through a square on the grid once.
- Lines on the route cannot cross.

Give your route to a friend and ask them to write the directions. Then check their directions. Were they right?

2

The Language of Maths

This grid can be used to write and solve secret messages!

Use the grid to read this message.

A1 F2 F2   A4 D3 C2 E1 A4
B4 C3   A3 E1 E1 B4
A1 B4
C1 F2 A1 A4 A4 F3 C3 C3 A3
D1 C3 C3 F3   A1 B4
D5 E5 C5 C5   B2 C3 C4 F3 A4

	A	B	C	D	E	F
6	4	5	6	7	8	9
5	y	z	0	1	2	3
4	s	t	u	v	w	x
3	m	n	o	p	q	r
2	g	h	i	j	k	l
1	a	b	c	d	e	f

The Language of Maths

Use the grid above to write your own secret message and give it to a friend to solve.

3

S&C Volume 2

The Maths Herald

Name:

Date:

anticlockwise

Let's Investigate

Take a piece of scrap paper.

Fold it in half.

Fold it in half again along the fold.

You now have a right angle tester.

Use your right angle tester to look for:

- right angles
- angles that are smaller than a right angle
- angles that are larger than a right angle.

Record your findings in a table:

Right angle	Smaller than a right angle	Larger than a right angle
table corner		

The Puzzler

Play this game with a friend.

You need:
- 6 counters:
  3 of one colour
  3 of another colour

- Decide who will use which colour counters.

- Take turns to put a counter on one of the islands. (But **not** the middle island.)

- Continue until all 6 counters are on the board.

- Now take turns to slide one of your counters along a bridge to the first empty island.

- The winner is the 1st person to get their 3 counters in a row, column or diagonal.

Play a total of 4 games, taking turns to place the 1st counter on the board.

Discuss with your friend strategies for winning the game.

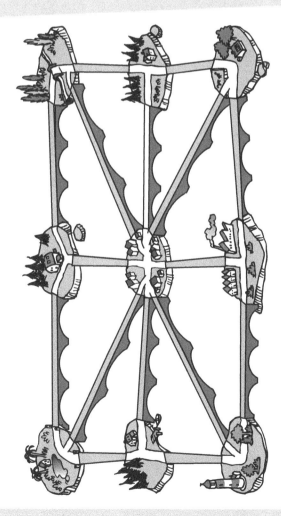

4

The Language of Maths

This sheet of paper has been turned 1 right angle clockwise.

This sheet of paper has been flipped over side to side.

How has each of these sheets of paper been turned or flipped?

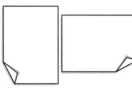

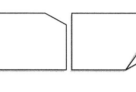

Let's Investigate

Work with a friend.

On a sheet of A4 paper, use a ruler to draw 2 straight lines from one side of the sheet to another side. Make sure that the 2 lines cross over each other.

Your lines might look like these:

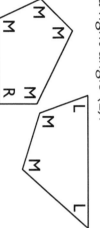
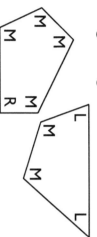

Now draw a 3rd line that crosses both the other lines.

Cut out the 7 shapes you have made.

Use the right angle tester you made in the Let's Investigate activity on page 1 to see if each of the angles in each shape is a right angle (R), more than a right angle (M), or less than a right angle (L).

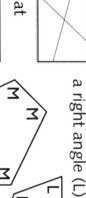

At Home

On your way from home to school one morning, count all the turns you make.

In the afternoon, count all the turns you make from school to home.

What pattern do you notice?

On another day, on your way from home to school, count all the turns you make to the right, and all the turns you make to the left.

In the afternoon, on your way from school to home, count all the turns you make to the right, and all the turns you make to the left.

What patterns do you notice?

The Language of Maths

A turn on this wheel from A to B can be described in these different ways:

- a quarter turn clockwise
- 1 right angle clockwise
- a quarter turn to the right
- 1 right angle to the right

Describe the turns between these points:

- From A to C
- From B to C
- From A to D
- From D to A
- From C to D
- From C to A
- From D to B
- From B to D
- From B to A
- From D to C
- From C to B

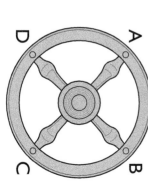

The Maths Herald

Name:

Date:

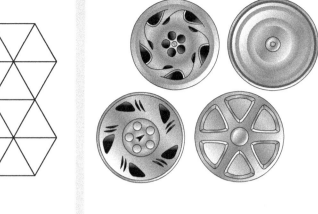

The Puzzler

rotate

How many hexagons can you see?

Let's Investigate

Investigate the different shapes and patterns of the hubcaps on car wheels.

Make drawings of the different patterns.

Now sort your patterns.

Can you sort them a different way?

Construct

Cut out the squares on the sheet.

Using the lines on the squares as sides and corners, it is possible to make a square.

Arrange the sides and the corners to make the following shapes:

- rectangle
- pentagon
- hexagon
- octagon

At Home

The next time you visit the supermarket make a list of all the items you can find that are either cuboids or cylinders.

You should find lots!

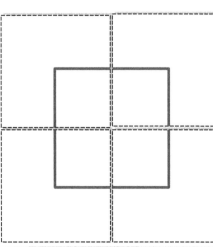

Construct

Origami is the Japanese art of paper folding.

Follow these instructions to make a triangular box.

You will need 3 sheets of coloured square paper.

Step 1
Using 1 of the coloured squares, fold the paper in half.

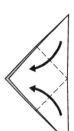

Step 2
Fold the top corners towards the bottom point and then open to show the folds.

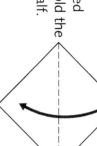

Step 3
Fold both layers of the bottom point to the top, then open.

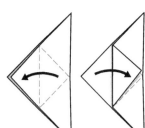
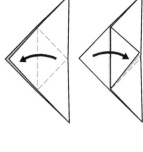

Step 4
This is one part of the box. Repeat Steps 1, 2 and 3 twice more, to make three of these altogether.

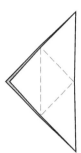

Step 5
Place one part inside the other.

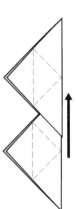

Step 6
Then link the 3 parts together.

Your finished box should look like this.

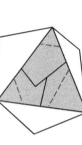

Looking for Patterns

Each of the shapes below goes into a machine and comes out slightly different.

Draw the last shape after it has come out of the machine.

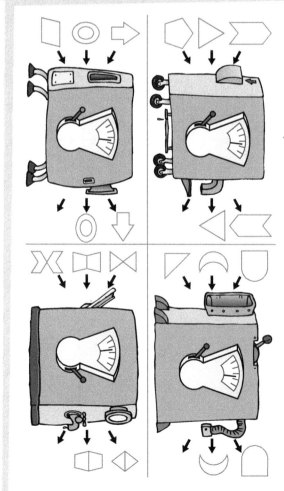

The Language of Maths

Starting at 'M', how many different ways can you follow the lines to spell the word 'MATHS'?

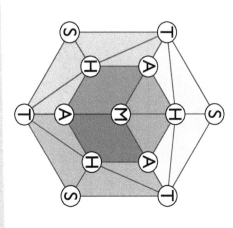

The Maths Herald

Name:

Date:

The Language of Maths

Sort these shapes into 2 groups.

Describe each group.

How else could you sort these shapes?

At Home

GIVE WAY

triangle

What shapes are used for road signs? Find as many different road signs as you can.

Draw a picture of each road sign and name the shape of the sign.

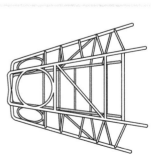

Sports Update

Look at the climbing frame in the gym or hall.

What different shapes can you see in the climbing frame?

Design your own climbing frame using as many different shapes as you can.

Label the shapes on your design.

Think about different climbing frames you may have visited in some parks.

Let's Investigate

A compass is an instrument used to find direction.

Make your own compass.

- Take a square sheet of paper and fold it in half.

- Then fold it in half again.

- Open out the paper and draw a cross and the 4 compass directions: north (N), south (S), east (E) and west (W).

Ask your teacher to show you the direction of north.

Place your paper compass in the correct position.

Find some things in your classroom that you can see in each direction.

Why not take your paper compass outside and do the same thing?

Construct

0 1 2 3 4 5 6 7 8 9

The digits 0 and 1 have been made using squares and triangles.

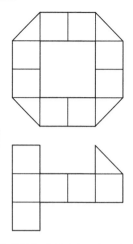

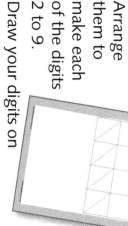

Cut out the shapes on the sheet.

Arrange them to make each of the digits 2 to 9.

Draw your digits on squared paper.

direction

Let's Investigate

Look at the TV listings in a newspaper or magazine.

Choose any day.

How many right angles does the minute hand turn through during different programmes?

15 minutes or $\frac{1}{4}$ hour

30 minutes or $\frac{1}{2}$ hour

45 minutes or $\frac{3}{4}$ hour

60 minutes or 1 hour

Record your results in a table.

Programme	Start time	Finish time	Number of right angles

The Puzzler

The diagrams below are all made from matchsticks.

Make each shape then follow the instructions.

Draw your results on squared dot paper.

Remove 1 match to make 3 squares.

Remove 4 matches to make 5 squares.

Remove 2 matches to make 2 squares.

Move 2 matches to make 2 squares.

Construct

Draw a plan of your school playground.

Try and draw your plan to scale.

If you could change 5 things about your school playground what would they be?

Show these on your plan.

The Maths Herald

Name:

Date:

The Language of Maths

How many questions can you ask a friend without them answering 'yes' or 'no'?

Make a list of suitable questions. Here are some to get you started.

- Are you 7 years old?
- You know I am.
- Do you have any brothers or sisters?
- I do.
- Are you in Year 2?
- Of course.
- Is today Wednesday?
- No. Oh!

Choose a friend and tell them that you are going to ask them some questions.

They must answer you as quickly as possible, without saying the words 'yes' or 'no'.

Keep a tally of how many questions your friend answers before saying 'yes' or 'no'.

Repeat, asking other friends.

For most people, how many questions did you ask before they answered 'yes' or 'no'?

Focus on Science

To stay fit and healthy we should eat 5 portions of fruit or vegetables every day.

Keep a record of the fruit and vegetables you eat in a week. Show your results in a table.

The Language of Maths

A test paper asked 4 questions about this graph.

On the right are Rosie's answers.

What might the 4 questions have been?

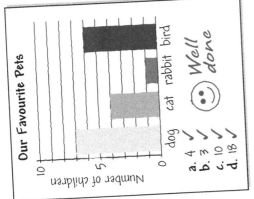

Our Favourite Pets

Number of children

dog   cat   rabbit   bird

a. 4
b. 3
c. 10
d. 18

Well done

tally

At Home

Look around your room.

How many different colours can you find?

Find examples of as many different colours as you can.

Draw a tally chart similar to the one on the right to record your findings.

Colour	Tally	Number

🌐 Around the World

The city of Detroit is the potato capital of the USA.

Each person in Detroit eats about 70 bags of crisps each year!

Most Americans eat about 45 bags of crisps a year.

How many bags of crisps do you eat in a year?

How many bags of crisps do most children in your school eat in a year?

Follow these steps:

Step 1: Plan what to do

Step 2: Collect the information

Step 3: Think about the information

Step 4: Present the information

Step 5: Discuss the results

🎨 The Arts Roundup

Leo, Kevin and Sam are friends. One plays the piano, one the flute and another the violin.

The child who plays the flute is the youngest.

Kevin is older than the piano player.

The piano player's brothers and sisters also all learn the piano.

Leo doesn't have any brothers and sisters.

Which friend plays which instrument?

Use the diagram to help you.

	piano	flute	violin
Leo			
Kevin			
Sam			

🔬 Focus on Science

Roll a toy car down a slope.

What happens as the slope gets steeper?

What happens when your toy car has a heavy load?

Does it go as fast? Does it go as far?

Write about what you find out.

Now roll the toy car down different surfaces.

On which ones does it go fastest?

On which ones does it go further?

What happens if the toy car has a heavy load? Is there a difference?

Write about what you find out.

How many people are you going to experiment on?

Write about your experiment and your results.

Be prepared to explain your results.

💡 Let's Investigate

Your writing hand is better at picking up things than your other hand.

True or false?

Design an experiment to find out whether this is true or not.

What are you going to need?

Who are you going to experiment on?

The Maths Herald

Name:

Date:

Technology Today

Technology refers to machines and equipment that help to make our lives easier.

Look around your classroom and throughout the school.

Make a list of all the different examples of technology you can find.

Computers and calculators are 2 obvious examples. Can you find less obvious examples?

When you have finished, compare your list with a friend to make 1 big list.

Then sort your list.

Write about how you sorted the technology.

How else could you sort your list?

Around the World

Look through a selection of travel magazines and design a poster for a travel agency advertising a holiday.

Include on your poster the cost of the holiday and what's included in the price.

Think about what other information might be useful to include on your poster.

Let's Investigate

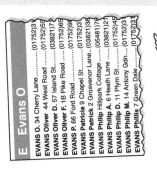

In a white pages telephone directory, telephone numbers are organised according to the first letter in a person's last name – their surname.

Look through a telephone directory.

- Which letter of the alphabet is the most common letter for the first letter of a person's surname?

- Which is the least common letter?

- Look back at the most common letter. What is the most common name in the telephone directory starting with this letter?

- What else can you find out about the names in a telephone directory?

E   Evans O

EVANS O. 34 Cherry Lane .... (01752)3
EVANS Oliver 44 West Road .... (01752)55
EVANS Oliver D. 57 Island St. ...... (0382117
EVANS Oliver F. 1B Pike Road ...... (01752)65
EVANS P. 66 Ford Road .... (01752)9
EVANS Patricia 9 Chapel St. .... (01752)3
EVANS Patrick 2 Grosvenor Lane... (03821)38
EVANS Philip Hillpark Cottage ...... (05481)7
EVANS Philip A. 6 Heath Lane ...... (03821)2
EVANS Philip D. 11 Plym St. .... (01752)4
EVANS Phillip M. 14 Antony Gdn ... (01752)3
EVANS Phillis 7 Green Dale .... (01752)3

axes

The Language of Maths

Look at this block graph.

What might it be about?

Label the graph.

Write 3 statements about the graph.

Sports Update

Choose 5 friends.

How many times can each friend hop on one foot before they have to put their other foot back on the ground or they fall over?

Record how many times each friend hops.

Using squared paper, draw a graph like the one on the right to show how many times each friend hopped.

Think carefully about how you are going to label your graph.

253, 254, 255.

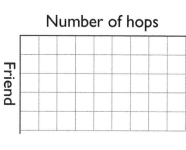

Number of hops

Friend

At Home

This weekend, spend some time looking for bugs!

How many different insects, spiders and other bugs can you find?

Keep a tally of all the different bugs you can find.

Draw a tally chart similar to the one on the right to record your findings.

Don't touch the bugs

Bug	Tally	Number

2

The Arts Roundup

What is your favourite type of film?

Find out the most popular type of film in your class.

Step 1: Plan what to do
Step 2: Collect the information
Step 3: Think about the information
Step 4: Present the information
Step 5: Discuss the results

How might the results change if you asked the children in Year 6?

What about a group of adults?

Why not find out?

Types of film

Action & Adventure
Cartoon
Comedy
Crime & Thriller
Documentary
Drama
Horror
Musical
Romance
Science fiction
Western

Technology Today

Do most children in your school wear:

- a watch with hands (it is called an analogue watch)?
- a digital watch?
- no watch at all?

Are the results the same for the whole school, or is it different for different year groups? Write about your results and what you did to get these results.

3

The Maths Herald

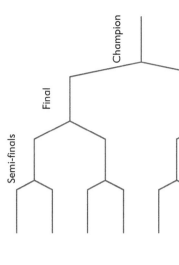

Name:

Date:

Sports Update

Noughts and Crosses Tournament

Round   Semi-finals   Final   Champion

Your class has been chosen to take part in the World Junior Noughts and Crosses Tournament. But you are only allowed to enter 1 child into the tournament.

To decide who this will be, you need to choose 8 friends to take part in your own class Noughts and Crosses Tournament.

Write the 8 names under the 'Round' heading.

Each pair plays 5 games of noughts and crosses. The 4 winners then move into the Semi-finals.

Again both pairs play 5 games and the 2 winners move to the final.

The final pair play 5 games and the winner is crowned the champion!

At Home

Look around your room.

How many different colours do you see?

Write these colours along the bottom of the graph.

Complete the block graph by colouring 1 block on the graph for each object of that colour.

Give your graph a name.

Number of objects

Colour

The Arts Roundup

A group of actors are putting on a play.

This morning they have all been out selling tickets.

The table shows how many tickets each actor sold.

 1 ticket

Name	Number of tickets sold
Leroy	🎟🎟🎟🎟🎟🎟
Sam	🎟🎟🎟🎟
Tom	🎟🎟🎟🎟🎟🎟🎟🎟
Paul	🎟🎟🎟🎟🎟
Jo	🎟🎟🎟🎟🎟🎟🎟🎟🎟🎟🎟

Write some sentences about how many tickets the actors sold today.

The Language of Maths

Look at the picture below.

It has been drawn using a special code called a glyph.

The picture tells us a story about someone.

Using the code on the right, write what you know about the person.

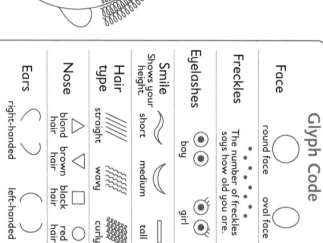

Glyph Code

Face	round face	oval face
Freckles	The number of freckles says how old you are.	
Eyelashes	boy	girl
Smile
Shows your height.	short	medium	tall
Hair type	straight	wavy	curly
Nose	blond hair	brown hair	black hair	red hair
Ears	right-handed		left-handed

Construct

Look at the activity above.

Use the code to draw 2 pictures; one of yourself and one of someone else in your class.

When you have drawn your pictures, give the one that you drew of someone else in your class to a friend. Can they discover who the picture is of?

classify

Let's Investigate

What is your favourite subject?

Colour a square on the graph to show this.

Ask other children in your class what their favourite subject is.

Show this on the graph.

We love music

Our favourite subject

Subject												
English												
Maths												
Science												
Music												
Art												
PE / Sport												
	1	2	3	4	5	6	7	8	9	10	11	12

Number of children

The Language of Maths

Look at the graph in the Let's Investigate activity above.

Write some sentences about your class's favourite subjects.

PE Rules

Teacher's notes

<table>
<tr><td>

Prerequisites for learning

- Read and write numbers to at least 100 in numerals and in words
- Recognise the place value of each digit in a two-digit number (tens, ones)
- Compare and order numbers from 0 up to 100
- Describe and extend number sequences
- Identify, represent and estimate numbers using different representations
- Use place value and number facts to solve problems
- Use a calculator

</td><td>

Resources

pencil and paper

Resource sheet 2: My notes (optional)

Resource sheet 3: Pupil self assessment booklet (optional)

selection of different newspapers and magazines

set of 0 – 9 digit cards (optional)

counters

interlocking cubes

calculator

</td></tr>
</table>

Teaching support

Page 1

Let's Investigate

- Encourage the children to look for numbers other than whole numbers, such as decimals, percentages and fractions. Are they able to explain what each of the numbers means? Are they able to arrange these numbers in order?

Looking for Patterns

- Children should not have any difficulty in identifying the rules for the first two patterns. However, for the third and fourth patterns, you may need to tell them that each of these patterns involves two operations.
- Tell the children that the third pattern involves multiplication and addition; and that the fourth pattern involves multiplication and subtraction.
- For each of the four patterns, ask the children to apply the rule to three other numbers.

Page 2

In the Past

- It is recommended that children work in pairs for this activity so that they can share ideas and discuss their reasoning.
- Once pairs have completed this activity, arrange a group discussion for pairs of children to share their ideas.

Looking for Patterns

- Ensure that children are familiar with the term 'approximately' and that they make an estimate before they count the actual number of ladybirds and spots.
- Once the children have completed this activity discuss with them how they arrived at their estimate.

Page 3

Looking for Patterns

- Ensure that children are familiar with the term 'digit' and that they understand that 0, 1, 2, 3, 4, 5, 6, 7, 8 and 9 are the ten digits that make up our number system.
- Discuss with the children that unless otherwise stated, some of the numbers in the box may be numbers in which one of the digits occurs more than once, for example, 112 or 909.
- Provide the children with two sets of 0 – 9 digit cards. They can use these cards to help them identify the three-digit numbers in the box.

The Arts Roundup

• Suggest the children draw a diagram, e.g.

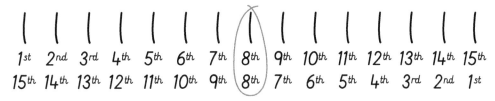

Page 4

Let's Investigate

• Before children use counters and cubes to carry out this investigation make sure they realise that they have to make approximations first.

• Children need to work in pairs for this activity, not only to carry out the experimental aspect, but also to share ideas and discuss their reasoning as to whether they can hold twice as much, more than twice as much or less than twice as much in two hands.

Technology Today

• This activity is designed to introduce children to number sequences using the constant function on the calculator. Different types of calculators operate slightly differently, but the most common method is to key in, for example:

 and then keep pressing the key.

AfL

• What does this number read?
• Which of these numbers is the largest / smallest?
• Tell me a number that lies between these two numbers.
• How would you write this number as a word / numeral?
• What is the rule for this pattern? How do you know this?
• Tell me two other numbers that have this rule.
• What are the advantages / disadvantages of having coins instead of notes?
• Would it be a good idea to have coins instead of notes for £20 and £50? Why not?
• *Point and ask:* Approximately how many spots are there on this many ladybirds? What about this many?
• How did you work out the answer to this problem / puzzle?
• What were the results of your experiment?
• What happens when you press these keys on a calculator?

Answers

Page 1

Let's Investigate
Results of the investigation will vary.

Looking for Patterns
Rule: Add 4 to the hat number.

Rule: Subtract 6 from the hat number.

Rule: Double the hat number and add 1.

Rule: Multiply the hat number by 10 and subtract 1.

Page 2

In the Past
Reasoning will vary.

Looking for Patterns
There are 32 ladybirds on the leaf.
There are 144 spots altogether.

Page 3

Looking for Patterns
The smallest number you can make using each digit only once is 102.

The largest number you can make using each digit only once is 987.

The smallest odd number is 101.

The largest even number is 998.

The largest number that has a 1 and an 8 is 981.

The smallest number that has a 2 and a 6 is 126.

The Arts Roundup
There are 15 members of The Imperial Ballet Company.

Page 4

Let's Investigate
Results of the investigation will vary.

Technology Today
Results of the investigation will vary.

Inquisitive ant

approximation
A figure or amount that is not exact, but may be slightly more or less in number or quantity.

Issue 2

Number

Prerequisites for learning

- Read and write numbers to at least 100 in numerals and in words
- Recognise the place value of each digit in a two-digit number (tens, ones)
- Describe and extend number sequences
- Identify, represent and estimate numbers using different representations
- Use place value and number facts to solve problems
- Recognise, find, name and write a half
- Solve logic puzzles

Resources

pencil and paper
Resource sheet 2: My notes (optional)
Resource sheet 3: Pupil self assessment booklet (optional)
Resource sheet 21: Squared dot paper
Resource sheet 22: Triangular dot paper (optional)
A3 paper
0 – 9 digit cards (optional)
counters

Teaching support

Page 1

Let's Investigate

- Ask the children to investigate how their results would differ for children in different classes, e.g. Foundation stage and Year 6.

Let's Investigate

- Ensure that the children understand what the term 'the sum of the digits is 4' means, i.e. 112 = 1 + 1 + 2 = 4.
- Do the children realise that they only need to use the digits 0 – 4 and not the digits 5 to 9?
- Provide the children with two sets of 0 – 4 digit cards.

Page 2

Looking for Patterns

- To help identify the rule for each sequence, suggest the children look at the difference between consecutive numbers in the sequence, e.g.

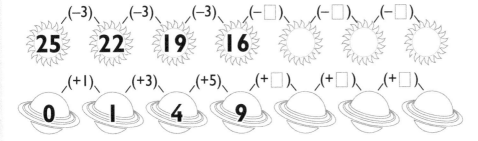

The Language of Maths

- You may wish to introduce the children to a logic diagram to help them solve the problem, i.e.

	8	9	10
Lisa	✗	✗	✓
Gary	✓	✗	✗
John	✗	✓	✗

Page 3

Looking for Patterns

- Suggest the children look at the patterns occurring in each of the columns in the 1 – 100 number square. What do they notice about the ones digits in each column? What about the tens digits?

Looking for Patterns

- This practical activity is designed to introduce children to triangular numbers.
- Children write down the first 10 triangular numbers.

Page 4

Looking for Patterns

- Ensure children do not count the total number of dots inside each shape. Remind them they are only expected to make estimates.
- For the first part of this activity, children are only required to look at the five shapes and order them, starting with the shape they think has the most dots in it.
- For the second part of this activity, children need to estimate the number of dots inside each shape.

Let's Investigate

- Children repeat the investigation using Resource sheet 22: Triangular dot paper.

AfL

- How did you work out the fewest number of sheets of large paper you would need for everyone to be able to stand on?
- Can you tell me some three-digit numbers where the sum of the digits is 5 / 6 / 7 / 8 … 25 / 26 / 27?
- What is the rule for this pattern? How do you know? What are the next three numbers in this pattern?
- Starting with a different first number, use this rule to write a sequence of 10 numbers.
- How did you work out the answer to this problem / solution to this puzzle?
- Without counting, how did you work out the values of the two question marks? What patterns did you notice?
- What is the special name given to these numbers? Can you see why it is called this?

Answers

Page 1

Let's Investigate
Results of the investigation will vary.

Let's Investigate
Conroy is incorrect. It is only possible to make 10 different three-digit numbers, i.e. 103, 112, 121, 130, 202, 211, 220, 301, 310, 400.

Page 2

Looking for Patterns
25, 22, 19, 16, 13, 10, 7
(Rule: Subtract 3)

3, 11, 19, 27, 35, 43, 51
(Rule: Add 8)

$\frac{1}{2}$, 1, $1\frac{1}{2}$, 2, $2\frac{1}{2}$, 3, $3\frac{1}{2}$
(Rule: Add $\frac{1}{2}$)

1, 2, 4, 7, 11, 16, 22
(Rule: Add 1, 2, 3, 4, …)

0, 1, 4, 9, 16, 25, 36
(Rule: Add 1, 3, 5, 7, …)

20, 19, 17, 16, 14, 13, 11, 10
(Rule: Subtract 1, Subtract 2, Subtract 1, Subtract 2, …)

The Language of Maths
Lisa is 10, Gary is 8 and John is 9.

Page 3

Looking for Patterns
? = 63
?? = 95

Looking for Patterns
3, 6, 10, 15, 21.
These are the first five triangular numbers.

Page 4

Looking for Patterns

A	C	B	E	D
Most dots				Least dots

Accept estimates around the following:

116	55	69	48	52
A	B	C	D	E

Let's Investigate
Results of the investigation will vary.

Inquisitive ant

digit
A numeral from 0 to 9.

Issue 3

Number

Prerequisites for learning

- Read and write numbers to at least 100 in numerals and in words
- Recognise the place value of each digit in a two-digit number (tens, ones)
- Describe and extend number sequences
- Compare and order numbers from 0 up to 100
- Make estimations and approximations
- Use lists, tables and diagrams to sort objects; explain choices using appropriate language, including 'not'

Resources

pencil and paper
Resource sheet 2: My notes (optional)
Resource sheet 3: Pupil self assessment booklet (optional)
Resource sheet 4: 1 – 100 number cards
calculator (optional)
Resource sheet 5: Six card puzzle
Resource sheet 19: 1 cm squared paper (optional)
set of 1 – 100 number cards or
simple percussion instrument, e.g. triangle, chime bar, hand bell, ...
set of 0 – 9 digit cards
selection of different newspapers
computer with internet access

Teaching support

Page 1

Looking for Patterns

- Children do not necessarily have to write lists containing all the numbers from 1 – 100 for the different sorting criteria they have used. It may be sufficient to just ask the children to name the criterion used, e.g.
  - odd number, even number
  - a multiple of 10, not a multiple of 10
  - a one-digit number, a two-digit number, a three-digit number.
- If there are insufficient packs of 1 – 100 number cards provide the children with cards made using the four sheets from Resource sheet 4: 1 – 100 number cards.
- Encourage children to sort the cards into three or more different groups, i.e. multiples of two, multiples of three, not a multiple of two or three.
- Once pairs of children have completed the activity, arrange them into groups of four to compare and discuss the different criteria they used for sorting the cards.

Technology Today

- You may wish to allow the children to use 1 cm squared paper to record each of the digits.
- Provide the children with a calculator to help them identify the arrangements of the seven light bars for each of the digits.
- Assist the children with drawing each of the digits in digital form by working with them on one or two of the digits, e.g.

5 light bars   3 light bars

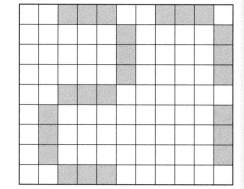

Page 2

The Arts Roundup

- The main focus of this activity is for children to record their simple rhythmic pattern using appropriate and meaningful symbols. Before the children go off to work independently on this activity you may wish to discuss with them the possible methods of recording. For example, a rhythmic pattern made using a triangle may be expressed as follows:

△△   △   △   △△△   △△   △

   (short   (long   (short   (long   (short
   pause)   pause)   pause)   pause)   pause)

NOTE: The length of space between symbols may be a way of distinguishing between the length of a pause between symbols.

- It is recommended that you provide the children with a sheet of 1 cm squared paper (Resource sheet 19) to help them record their rhythmic pattern.

The Language of Maths

- Children can investigate the meaning of each of the words and the prefix 'tri' on the internet.
- Children investigate words such as 'bicycle', 'biannual' and 'biplane'.

Page 3

The Puzzler

- If children are experiencing difficulty in identifying the rule (the number refers to the number of letters in each word) then draw their attention to one or two of the examples in the issue, for example:

Z E R O = 4   O N E = 3

① ② ③ ④   ① ② ③

At Home

- If the children are not familiar with tally marks, you may need to discuss this with them, before they undertake this investigation at home.
- Once the children have completed the investigation, ensure that there is an opportunity in class for pairs or groups of children to discuss their results.
- Children investigate who in their family receives the most telephone calls in a week.

Page 4

The Language of Maths

- Children can work in pairs or small groups on this activity.
- Referring to different pages in the newspaper, ask the children to comment on approximately what fraction of the page contains news or other stories or information / advertisements / photos / illustrations …

The Puzzler

- Once the children have tried the puzzle several times discuss with them the strategies they developed to improve their performance.

AfL

- How did you sort the number cards? What other ways did you sort them? How might you sort the cards into five groups? What criteria could you use?
- How many light bars are needed to make the number 27? What about 132?
- Tell me a number that uses 10 light bars. What about 12 light bars?
- How did you record your rhythmic pattern?
- What do all these words have in common? What parts of these words tell us this?
- How did you work out the solution to this puzzle?
- What can you tell me about the number of pages in a newspaper that give us information to do with sports? What about news?
- Approximately what fraction of this page has photos / illustrations / advertisements?

Answers

Page 1

Looking for Patterns
Criteria will vary.

Technology Today

6 light bars | 2 light bars | 5 light bars | 5 light bars | 4 light bars | 5 light bars | 6 light bars | 3 light bars | 7 light bars | 6 light bars

Answers may vary for different calculators.

Page 2

The Arts Roundup
Methods of recording will vary.

The Language of Maths
Prefix 'tri' means three of something.

Page 3

The Puzzler
FOUR = 4
FIVE = 4
SIX = 3
SEVEN = 5
EIGHT = 5
NINE = 4
TEN = 3
The number refers to the number of letters in each word.

At Home
Results of the investigation will vary.

Page 4

The Language of Maths
Results of the investigation will vary.

The Puzzler
No answers required.

Inquisitive ant

order
The way in which numbers, quantities or objects are arranged according to a particular pattern, sequence or method such as their relative value or size.

Prerequisites for learning

- Read and write numbers to at least 100 in numerals and in words
- Recognise the place value of each digit in a two-digit number (tens, ones)
- Describe and extend number sequences
- Compare and order numbers from 0 up to 100
- Make estimations and approximations
- Identify, represent and estimate numbers using different representations
- Use place value and number facts to solve problems
- Solve logic puzzles

Resources

pencil and paper
Resource sheet 2: My notes (optional)
Resource sheet 3: Pupil self assessment booklet (optional)
Resource sheet 6: 1 – 100 number squares (optional)
Resource sheet 19: 1 cm squared paper
Resource sheet 20: 2 cm squared paper
ruler
set of 0 – 9 digit cards
counters
stopwatch (optional)

Teaching support

Page 1

Let's Investigate

- Ensure children understand what a palindromic number is.
- Draw children's attention to the pattern of palindromic numbers from 100 to 300. If necessary, complete with them the palindromic numbers from 300 to 400:

101	111	121	131	141	151	161	171	181	191
202	212	222	232	242	252	262	272	282	292
303	313	323	333	343	353	363	373	383	393

- Suggest the children draw a table, similar to that above and in the Answers, to record all the numbers.
- Tell the children that there are 90 palindromic numbers between 100 and 1000.

Page 2

The Language of Maths

- Ensure the children realise that there are two parts to this activity. The first part involves each child writing down their own name as many times as they can in one minute. The second part involves both children writing down the same name as many times as they can in one minute.
- Remind the children that before they undertake either part of this activity they must first make a prediction.
- Before the children test their predictions you may wish to discuss with them their reasoning as to who will write their name more times, and why they think there will be different results when each child writes down the same name.

The Puzzler

- Suggest the children do this activity using a pencil as they may need to complete it using trial and improvement.
- Tell the children that there are six vertical groups of three numbers and six horizontal groups of three numbers.

Page 3

Looking for Patterns

- Encourage the children to work out how many squares there are in shapes 8, 9 and 10 by referring to the table and applying the rule rather than having to draw the shapes.

The Puzzler

- Ensure that children are aware of arrangements that are similar because of rotations, e.g.

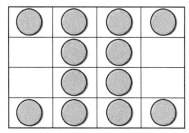 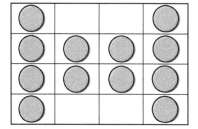

Page 4

Looking for Patterns

- Suggest the children draw a table to help them record the total number of digits required.

0	1	2	3	4	5	6	7	8	9

- If appropriate, provide the children with a 1 – 100 number square (Resource sheet 6: 1 – 100 number squares).
- If necessary, tell the children that each of the digits 2 – 9 occur the same number of times on the 1 – 100 number square. However, the digits 1 and 0 each occur a different number of times.

The Puzzler

- Once the children have tried the puzzle several times, discuss with them the strategies they developed to improve their performance.

- What are the palindromic numbers between 200 and 300? How did knowing these numbers help you work out how many palindromic numbers there are to 1000? What is the pattern to finding all these numbers?
- Did you manage to circle all the numbers on the grid?
- How did you know how many squares there were in the 8th, 9th and 10th shape? What was the pattern / rule?
- Did you recognise any patterns that helped you to see different ways that the counters could be arranged on the grid? What were they?
- How many 2s are there on a 1 – 100 number square? Are there this many 3s / 7s / 9s? What about zeros / ones?
- Did you get better at being able to order the cards? Why do you think this was?

Answers

Page 1

Let's Investigate

(11) (22) (33) (44) (55) (66) (77) (88) (99)

101	111	121	131	141	151	161	171	181	191
202	212	222	232	242	252	262	272	282	292

An explanation of the patterns noticed will vary.

303	313	323	333	343	353	363	373	383	393
404	414	424	434	444	454	464	474	484	494
505	515	525	535	545	555	565	575	585	595
606	616	626	636	646	656	666	676	686	696
707	717	727	737	747	757	767	777	787	797
808	818	828	838	848	858	868	878	888	898
909	919	929	939	949	959	969	979	989	999

Page 2

The Language of Maths
Results of the investigation will vary.

The Puzzler

17	9	18	22	10	28
23	2	51	60	33	71
45	42	49	83	40	99
31	28	35	32	46	67
85	55	45	13	42	80
93	71	62	50	51	53

Page 3

Looking for Patterns

1	2	3	4	5	6	7	8	9	10
1	3	5	7	9	11	13	15	17	19

The Puzzler
Answers will vary.
Two possible solutions include:

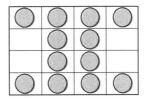 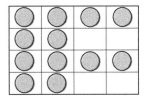

Page 4

Looking for Patterns

0	1	2	3	4	5	6	7	8	9
11	21	20	20	20	20	20	20	20	20

The Puzzler
No answer required.

Inquisitive ant prediction
To make a statement about the result of something based on given facts.

Issue 5

Addition

Prerequisites for learning

- Describe patterns and relationships involving numbers
- Recall and use addition and subtraction facts to 20 fluently, and derive and use related facts up to 100
- Use knowledge of number facts and operations to estimate and check answers to calculations
- Add numbers using concrete objects, pictorial representations, and mentally, including:
  - a two-digit number and ones
  - a two-digit number and tens
  - two two-digit numbers
  - adding three one-digit numbers
- Understand that subtraction is the inverse of addition and vice versa; use this to derive and record related addition and subtraction number sentences and to solve missing number problems
- Use the symbols + and = to record and interpret number sentences

Resources

pencil and paper

Resource sheet 2: My notes (optional)

Resource sheet 3: Pupil self assessment booklet (optional)

Resource sheet 6: 1 – 100 number squares (optional)

Resource sheet 20: 2 cm squared paper

ruler

calculator

Teaching support

Page 1

Focus on Science

- Ensure children realise that some of the animals can be birds.
- If appropriate, work through one or two examples with the children before they go off to work independently on this activity. For example:
  - If there were 2 chickens, 2 pigs and 2 goats in the field then the calculation would be: 2 + 2 + 4 + 4 + 4 + 4 = 20 legs.
  - If there were 3 chickens and 3 pigs in the field then the calculation would be: 2 + 2 + 2 + 4 + 4 + 4 = 18 legs.
- Suggest the children draw simple diagrams to represent their combinations of animals.

Page 2

Let's Investigate

- If necessary, provide children with a 1 – 100 number square from Resource sheet 6: 1 – 100 number squares.
- It is recommended that children do this activity, and the 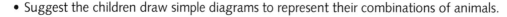 Let's Investigate activity that follows, during the same session as they both involve looking at the patterns and relationships on a 1 – 100 number square.
- It is also recommended that children work in pairs for this activity so that they can share ideas and discuss their reasoning.
- As the main focus of this activity is about exploring patterns and relationships and not calculating, allow the children to use a calculator to assist them.
- Ask the children to investigate the difference between the sum of the four numbers below a number on a 1 – 100 number square and the sum of the four numbers to the left of the number. (The difference is always 110.)
- Ask the children to investigate the difference between the sum of the five numbers below a number on a 1 – 100 number square and the sum of the five numbers to the left of the number. (The difference is always 165.)

Let's Investigate

- If necessary, provide children with a 1 – 100 number square from Resource sheet 6: 1 – 100 number squares.
- It is recommended that children do this activity, and the Let's Investigate activity above, during the same session as they both involve looking at the patterns and relationships on a 1 – 100 number square.
- It is also recommended that children work in pairs for this activity so that they can share ideas and discuss their reasoning.
- As the main focus of this activity is about exploring patterns and relationships and not calculating, allow the children to use a calculator to assist them.

Page 3

The Language of Maths

- Ensure that children have correctly assigned the values for each of the letters of the alphabet before working out the number of points that their name and other names are worth.
- Ask the children to find a name that has a total of 20 / 32 / 50 … points.

The Puzzler

- Ensure that children understand how the first set of three grids work as they will need to know this before completing the second set of three grids and the first The Puzzler activity on page 4.
- Once the children have completed this activity, discuss with them their methods for completing the second set of three grids. If appropriate, discuss with them the inverse relationship between addition and subtraction.

Page 4

The Puzzler

- Ensure that children have understood and completed The Puzzler activity on page 3 before starting on this activity.
- If necessary, draw children's attention to the row of three ⭕ in the first puzzle. If 3 × ⭕ = 12, then ⭕ = 4. Similarly, the column of three ◎ in the second puzzle. If 3 × ◎ = 9, then ◎ = 3.

The Puzzler

- The main focus of this activity is the strategies that children develop as they play the games in order to help them win. Therefore, once pairs of children have played their four games, arrange the pairs into groups and discuss with the children the various strategies they used to help them win the game.

AfL

- What was the largest / fewest number of legs you managed to get for the six animals? What were the animals?
- Tell me one of the patterns on a 1 – 100 number square.
- Can you explain to me why this happens?
- What is the value of your name?
- Who in this class do you think has the name with the most points? Why do you think that is?
- Can you tell me a name that is worth between 20 and 30 points?
- How did you work out the missing numbers from these three puzzles? What about the numbers from these three puzzles?
- How did you work out the value of this symbol? How did you know that this symbol was a 4 / 3?

Answers

Page 1

Focus on Science
Answers will vary. However, totals will be between 12 and 24 legs.

Page 2

Let's Investigate
The difference between the sum of the two numbers below a number on a 1 – 100 number square and the sum of the two numbers to the left of the number is always 33.
For example:
(15 + 25) – (3 + 4)
= 40 – 7
= 33

3	4	5
13	14	15
23	24	25

The difference between the sum of the three numbers below a number on a 1 – 100 number square and the sum of the three numbers to the left of the number is always 66.
For example,
(15 + 25 + 35) – (2 + 3 + 4)
= 75 – 9
= 66

2	3	4	5
12	13	14	15
22	23	24	25
32	33	34	35

Let's Investigate
The sum of the two numbers either side of a number on a 1 – 100 number square is always the same as twice the number in the middle. For example:

11	12	13

11 + 13 = 24
12 × 2 = 24

The sum of the eight numbers that surround a number on a 1 – 100 number square is always the same as eight times the number in the middle. For example:
1 + 2 + 3 + 11 + 13 + 21 + 22 + 23 = 96
12 × 8 = 96

1	2	3
11	12	13
21	22	23

Page 3

The Language of Maths

A	B	C	D	E	F	G	H	I	J	K	L	M
1	2	3	4	5	6	7	8	9	10	11	12	13

N	O	P	Q	R	S	T	U	V	W	X	Y	Z
14	15	16	17	18	19	20	21	22	23	24	25	26

Names and their values will vary.

The Puzzler

8	5	(13)
4	7	(11)
(12)	(12)	24

6	3	(9)
9	2	(11)
(15)	(5)	20

12	4	(16)
6	7	(13)
(18)	(11)	29

3	7	(10)
5	10	(15)
(8)	(17)	25

8	6	(14)
2	3	(5)
(10)	(9)	19

9	5	(14)
4	11	(15)
(13)	(16)	29

Page 4

The Puzzler

5	4	3	(12)
4	4	4	(12)
6	2	2	(10)
(15)	(10)	(9)	34

3	7	7	(17)
3	7	4	(14)
3	5	6	(14)
(9)	(19)	(17)	45

The Puzzler
Strategies will vary.

Inquisitive ant  total
The sum of two or more numbers.

Issue 6

Addition

Prerequisites for learning

- Describe patterns and relationships involving numbers
- Recall and use addition and subtraction facts to 20 fluently, and derive and use related facts up to 100
- Use knowledge of number facts and operations to estimate and check answers to calculations
- Add numbers using concrete objects, pictorial representations, and mentally, including:
  - a two-digit number and ones
  - a two-digit number and tens
  - two two-digit numbers
  - adding three one-digit numbers
- Understand that subtraction is the inverse of addition and vice versa; use this to derive and record related addition and subtraction number sentences and to solve missing number problems
- Use the symbols + and = to record and interpret number sentences

Resources

pencil and paper

Resource sheet 2: My notes (optional)

Resource sheet 3: Pupil self assessment booklet (optional)

set of dominoes

four 1 – 6 dice (optional)

set of 1 – 9 digit cards (optional)

art paper

coloured pencils

Teaching support

Page 1

The Puzzler

- Some calculations have more than one possible answer. Can the children find them?

Looking for Patterns

- Draw children's attention to the illustration and discuss with them the strategy of finding pairs of numbers that total 10 or 20.
- Once the children have rewritten each of the calculations, as a group discuss the various mental calculation strategies that children used to make the calculations more effective and efficient.

Page 2

The Puzzler

- If necessary, tell the children one of the pairs of numbers and the total (see Answers).
- Once the children have completed the activity, as a group discuss the various mental calculation strategies children used to estimate which pairs of numbers when added together made one of the numbers on the beach huts.

Let's Investigate

- If appropriate, discuss with the children how a pair of two-digit numbers totals 100 if the tens digits total 90, and the ones digits total 10, for example:

  66 + 34
  = (60 + 30) + (6 + 4)
  = 90 + 10
  = 100

- Tell the children that there are at least 14 pairs of numbers that total 100 and four sets of three numbers that total 100. Can they find them all?

Page 3

Let's Investigate

- Tell the children that they will need at least three dominoes in each group.
- Do not allow the children to use a set of dominoes.

Looking for Patterns

- There are several aspects to this activity. Firstly, adding three numbers together. Secondly, identifying a pattern from the examples provided. Thirdly, being able to apply the pattern and finally offering an explanation as to how the activity was completed. Ensure that in their explanations children write about the patterns they noticed.

- Remind the children that the opposite sides of a 1 – 6 dice total 7.
- Allow the children to use three 1 – 6 dice.
- Children roll four 1 – 6 dice, work out the total of the four numbers on top and, before turning over the dice, say the total of the four numbers on the bottom.

Page 4

Let's Investigate

- Provide the children with one solution to get them started.
- Do the children recognise that, for the puzzle to work, only odd numbers can be placed in the middle of the pattern?

- Allow the children to use a set of 1 – 9 digit cards.
- Ask the children to arrange the digits so that the difference between the totals of the row and the column is 3, 5 or 7.

The Arts Roundup

- Tell the children that they must use at least three different shapes in each picture.
- Children draw pictures to values other than £1, e.g. £1.50 or £2.
- What if you included a ⬠ at 30p and / or a ⬡ at 15p?

```
            ┌───┐
            │ 2 │
            └───┘
            ┌───┐
            │ 7 │
            └───┘
┌───┐┌───┐┌───┐┌───┐┌───┐
│ 1 ││ 5 ││ 3 ││ 6 ││ 9 │
└───┘└───┘└───┘└───┘└───┘
            ┌───┐
            │ 8 │
            └───┘
            ┌───┐
            │ 4 │
            └───┘
```

AfL

- How did you work out which number belongs in this box? Did you guess or did you see a pattern? What was the pattern?
- What was the best way of working out the answer to this number sentence? Why do you think that this is the best way?
- How did you work out what two numbers to add together to make this total?
- 26 and what other number total 100? How did you work that out?
- How did you work out the total of the three numbers on the bottom of the dice?
- How many different ways did you find to arrange the cards? What patterns did you notice as you were finding different arrangements? How did this help you find other arrangements?

Answers

Page 1

The Puzzler

$\boxed{4} + \boxed{5} = 9$ $2\boxed{5} + 2\boxed{5} = \boxed{5}0$ $1\boxed{5} + 9 = 2\boxed{4}$

or $\boxed{5} + \boxed{4} = 9$

$\boxed{4}2 + \boxed{5}1 = 93$ $2\boxed{5} + \boxed{4}2 = 67$ $\boxed{4}3 + \boxed{4}2 = 8\boxed{5}$

or $\boxed{5}2 + \boxed{4}1 = 93$

Looking for Patterns
8 + 2 + 7 + 3 + 5 = 25
9 + 11 + 5 + 5 + 3 = 33
12 + 8 + 6 + 4 + 7 = 37
Answers may vary.

Page 2

The Puzzler
14 + 26 = 40   18 + 23 = 41   15 + 27 = 42
19 + 24 = 43   16 + 28 = 44   17 + 29 = 46

Let's Investigate
Pairs of numbers that total 100 include:
57 + 43   84 + 16   68 + 32   75 + 25   61 + 39
76 + 24   62 + 38   87 + 13   51 + 49   90 + 10
60 + 40   80 + 20   50 + 50   30 + 70

Three numbers that total 100 include:
45 + 32 + 23   42 + 34 + 24
46 + 43 + 11   51 + 35 + 14

Other calculations are possible.

Page 3

Let's Investigate
Results of the investigation will vary.

Looking for Patterns
Totals on top:
9   10   13   12
Totals on the bottom:
12   11   8   9
Explanations will vary.

Page 4

Let's Investigate
Answers will vary.

The Arts Roundup
Pictures will vary.

Inquisitive ant number sentence
Also referred to as a calculation. The written process for working out the answer to a mathematical problem.

Issue 7

Subtraction

Prerequisites for learning

- Describe patterns and relationships involving numbers
- Recall and use addition and subtraction facts to 20 fluently, and derive and use related facts up to 100
- Use knowledge of number facts and operations to estimate and check answers to calculations
- Subtract numbers using concrete objects, pictorial representations, and mentally, including:
  - a two-digit number and ones
  - a two-digit number and tens
  - two two-digit numbers
- Understand that subtraction is the inverse of addition and vice versa; use this to derive and record related addition and subtraction number sentences and to solve missing number problem
- Use the symbols – and = to record and interpret number sentences

Resources

pencil and paper
Resource sheet 2: My notes (optional)
Resource sheet 3: Pupil self assessment booklet (optional)
set of 0 – 9 digit cards
two 1 – 6 dice
counters

Teaching support

Page 1

Looking for Patterns

- An important aspect of this activity is knowing which calculation to start with, and the order in which to work through the five calculations in order to find each of the values of the missing digits.

- Tell the children the value of one or two of the missing digits (see Answers).

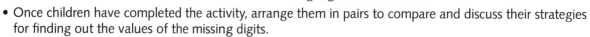

- Once children have completed the activity, arrange them in pairs to compare and discuss their strategies for finding out the values of the missing digits.

The Puzzler

- Discuss the following with the children:
  - the difference between two odd numbers is always an even number
  - the difference between two even numbers is always an even number
  - the difference between an odd number and an even number is always an odd number.
- Children are able to write one of the solutions to the puzzle on the issue. However, be aware that some children may need assistance with recording other solutions.

Page 2

The Puzzler

- If necessary, tell the children one of the pairs of numbers and the difference (see Answers).
- Once the children have completed the activity, as a group discuss the various mental calculation strategies children used to estimate which pairs of numbers have a difference that is one of the numbers on the cupboards.

Let's Investigate

- Work through an example with the children. Ensure they realise that for each set of three digit cards there are six different subtraction calculations possible, e.g.

  42 – 7 = 35

  24 – 7 = 17

114

$72 - 4 = 68$
$27 - 4 = 23$
$47 - 2 = 45$
$74 - 2 = 72$

Page 3

Let's Investigate

- Ensure that children realise that ☐ stands for an even digit and ◯ stands for an odd digit.
- What if the equation was ◯☐ – ☐◯ = ☐☐ or ◯◯ – ☐☐ = ◯☐ ?

The Puzzler

- Children repeat the activity following different routes from 20 to each of the diamonds, thus ending up with a different number in each of the diamonds.

Page 4

Let's Investigate

- Ensure that the children realise that they play the game by themselves. It is not until the second part of this activity, when children think about how to convert the activity into a game, that they work in pairs.

AfL

- How did you know which number cards belong to this calculation?
- How did you work out what numbers to write in connecting circles?
- How did you work out what two numbers have a difference of …?
- How many different subtraction number sentences can you make from these three digits?
- How did you work out the solution to this puzzle?
- How could you change the rules to make this into a game?

Answers

Page 1

Looking for Patterns

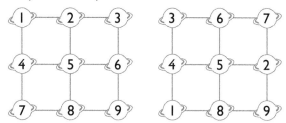

$$2\,\overset{\star}{0} - 6 = 1\,\overset{\star}{4} \qquad 1\,\overset{\star}{9} - 9 = \overset{\star}{1}\,0$$

$$1\,\overset{\star}{7} - \overset{\star}{8} = 9 \qquad 57 - 2\,\overset{\star}{6} = \overset{\star}{3}\,1$$

$$29 - \overset{\star}{2}\,\overset{\star}{5} = 4$$

The Puzzler
Many solutions are possible. Here are two:

Page 2

The Puzzler

36 – 15 = 21	35 – 13 = 22	39 – 16 = 23
34 – 10 = 24	37 – 12 = 25	38 – 11 = 27

Let's Investigate
Numbers and calculations will vary. However, for each set of three cards there should be six different subtraction calculations.

Page 3

Let's Investigate
Number sentences will vary.

The Puzzler
Results will vary.

Page 4

Let's Investigate
No answer required.

Inquisitive ant

difference
The amount by which one number or quantity is greater or smaller than another.

Subtraction

Prerequisites for learning

- Describe patterns and relationships involving numbers
- Recall and use addition and subtraction facts to 20 fluently, and derive and use related facts up to 100
- Use knowledge of number facts and operations to estimate and check answers to calculations
- Add and subtract numbers using concrete objects, pictorial representations, and mentally, including:
  - a two-digit number and ones
  - a two-digit number and tens
  - two two-digit numbers
  - adding three one-digit numbers
- Understand that subtraction is the inverse of addition and vice versa; use this to derive and record related addition and subtraction number sentences and to solve missing number problems
- Use the symbols +, − and = to record and interpret number sentences

Resources

pencil and paper

Resource sheet 2: My notes (optional)

Resource sheet 3: Pupil self assessment booklet (optional)

5p, 10p, 20p, 50p coins, real or play (optional)

set of 0 – 9 digit cards

Teaching support

Page 1

Money Matters

- Ensure that the children are confident with finding pairs of multiples of 5 and 10 that total 100, e.g. 25 + 75, 30 + 70.
- Tell the children that there are 15 different combinations of coins and amounts possible.

- Provide the children with a 5p, 10p, 20p, and 50p to allow them to find different combinations of coins.

The Puzzler

- Tell the children one (or more) of the numbers (see Answers).
- Tell the children that there are 10 different sets of four numbers possible. Can they find all 10 sets? What patterns do they notice?

Page 2

Technology Today

- What if there were different amounts of money in the centre of the machine, for example, £2, £1.20, £1.50, …?

The Puzzler

- You subtract a one-digit number from a two-digit number and get a one-digit answer, so the two-digit number must be 10, 11, 12 or a teen number. This means that C = 1. If you subtract 1 from a two-digit number and get a one-digit answer, then the two-digit number must be 10, so D = 0. This means that P = 9.

Page 3

The Puzzler
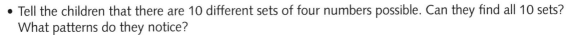
- Some calculations have more than one possible answer. Can the children find them?

Let's Investigate

- Remind the children that they can only use each digit once in each calculation.

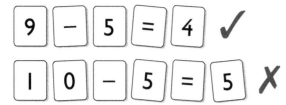

Page 4

Let's Investigate

- Remind the children that they will need to record all of their calculations.
- Ask the children to choose five or six digit cards and arrange them to make different combinations of two-digit and three-digit numbers. For example:

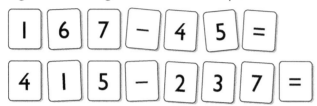

Money Matters

- If necessary, work through one of the possibilities with the children. For example:

  50p + 20p + 10p = 80p

- What amounts up to £1 could you make with two / three of these coins? What is the change from £1 for this amount?
- Tell me what the four numbers were in the box. How did you work out what numbers they were? Did you find another set of four numbers that could have been in the box?
- What amount do you end up with if you follow the trail to this circle?
- How did you work out the value of each of these letters?
- How did you work out which number belonged in this box? Did you guess or did you see a pattern? What was the pattern?
- What was the best way of working out the answer to this number sentence? Why do you think this is the best way?
- Tell me one of your clever number sentences that has an answer of five.
- Tell me one of the amounts of money that might be left in the purse.

Answers

Page 1

Money Matters

Coins	Amount	Change from £1
5p	5p	95p
10p	10p	90p
20p	20p	80p
50p	50p	50p
5p, 10p	15p	85p
5p, 20p	25p	75p
5p, 50p	55p	45p
10p, 20p	30p	70p
10p, 50p	60p	40p
20p, 50p	70p	30p
5p, 10p, 20p	35p	65p
5p, 10p, 50p	65p	35p
5p, 20p, 50p	75p	25p
10p, 20p, 50p	80p	20p
5p, 10p, 20p, 50p	85p	15p

The Puzzler
The four numbers can be any of the following combinations:
11, 24, 29 and 40.   16, 29, 34 and 45.
12, 25, 30 and 41.   17, 30, 35 and 46.
13, 26, 31 and 42.   18, 31, 36 and 47.
14, 27, 32 and 43.   19, 32, 37 and 48.
15, 28, 33 and 44.   20, 33, 38 and 49.
Other answers are possible.

Page 2

Technology Today

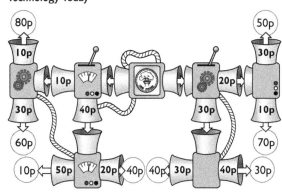

The Puzzler
C = 1, D = 0 and P = 9
10 − 1 = 9

Page 3

The Puzzler
1$\boxed{2}$ − $\boxed{3}$ = 9

$\boxed{2}$5 − 1$\boxed{3}$ = 1$\boxed{2}$
or $\boxed{2}$5 − 1$\boxed{2}$ = 1$\boxed{3}$

$\boxed{3}$6 − $\boxed{2}$8 = 8

57 − $\boxed{3}$1 = $\boxed{2}$6
or 57 − $\boxed{2}$1 = $\boxed{3}$6

4$\boxed{3}$ − 2$\boxed{4}$ = 19

$\boxed{3}$8 − 1$\boxed{3}$ = $\boxed{2}$5

Let's Investigate
Calculations will vary. However, ensure that each calculation contains the digit 5 / 9 and that no digit is used more than once.

Page 4

Let's Investigate
Numbers and calculations will vary.

Money Matters

Spend	Left
5p	80p
10p	75p
20p	65p
50p	35p

Spend	Left
10p	£1.70
20p	£1.60
50p	£1.30
£1	80p

Inquisitive ant  change (money)
1. Collection of coins.
2. The balance of money given back to a customer who has given a larger sum than the cost of the goods or services purchased.

Issue 9

Multiplication

Prerequisites for learning

- Understand that halving is the inverse of doubling and derive and recall doubles of all numbers to at least 20, and the corresponding halves
- Recall and use multiplication and division facts for the 2, 5 and 10 multiplication tables
- Recognise multiples of 2, 5 and 10
- Count in steps of 3 and 4 from 0 and begin to count from 0 in other single-digit steps
- Use knowledge of number facts and operations to estimate and check answers to calculations
- Represent repeated addition and arrays as multiplication
- Recall and use known multiplication facts to perform written and mental calculations
- Understand that division is the inverse of multiplication and vice versa; use this to derive and record related multiplication and division number sentences and to solve missing number problems
- Use the symbols × and = to record and interpret number sentences
- Solve logic puzzles

Resources

pencil and paper

Resource sheet 2: My notes (optional)

Resource sheet 3: Pupil self assessment booklet (optional)

Resource sheet 7: Squares

Resource sheet 20: 2 cm squared paper

counters (optional)

set of 0 – 9 digit cards

scissors

two different coloured pencils

Teaching support

Page 1

The Puzzler

- Once the children have completed the activity, as a group discuss the various mental calculation strategies children used to estimate which pairs of numbers when multiplied together make one of the products on the number cards.
- If necessary, suggest the children estimate which pairs of numbers multiply together to make one of the products on the cards by looking at the ones digit in each of the teen numbers in the balloons and multiplying this number by each of the digits in the baskets to see if the product is the ones digit of any of the numbers on the number card.
- If necessary, tell the children one of the pairs of numbers and the product (see Answers).

Let's Investigate

- Children need to understand the term 'multiple' before working on this activity and the two 🐜 Looking for Patterns activities on page 4. Therefore, it is recommended that the children complete the Inquisitive ant task before starting any of these three activities.
- While most children should be able to identify those numbers that are in the multiples of 3 list and the multiples of 4 list, they may have some difficulty in identifying that these numbers are multiples of 12.
- Discuss with the children the concept of 'common multiples'.

Page 2

Sports Update

- If necessary, work through one or two of the starting numbers with the children, i.e.

  $1 \times 2 = 2$ $2 \times 2 = 4$

  $2 - 1 = 1$ $4 - 1 = 3$

  $1 \times 2 = 2$ $3 \times 2 = 6$

  $2 - 1 = 1$ $6 - 1 = 5$

  $1 \times 2 = 2$ $5 \times 2 = 10$

  $2 \times 2 = 4$ $10 \times 2 = 20$

- Ask the children what pattern they notice in the final scores. (In the sequence of car numbers 1 to 6, each final score is 16 more than that of the previous car number.)

Let's Investigate

- Remind the children that they will need to record their numbers.

- Ensure the children realise that they cannot use the same digit twice when making pairs of numbers where one number is twice, three times or four times the other number. For example:

- Encourage the children to make two-digit and three-digit pairs of numbers. For example:

Page 3

Let's Investigate

- Work with the children to make one of the possible rectangles using 24 squares. Discuss the array with them and how it can be written as two multiplication calculations. For example:

$4 \times 6 = 24$

$6 \times 4 = 24$

If necessary, repeat using fewer squares.

- Once the children have completed the activity, discuss with the group which numbers of squares only make one array, i.e. prime numbers of squares.

Money Matters

- Ensure the children realise that the computer game the five friends are buying costs £30 and between them they have the right amount of money to buy the game.

- Suggest the children use 30 counters to represent £30 and use the counters to divide the money between the five friends.

Page 4

Looking for Patterns

- It is recommended that children have completed the Inquisitive ant task and the Let's Investigate activity on page 1 before starting on this activity.
- Ensure the children realise that the paths only go vertically or horizontally and not diagonally. Also tell the children that the two paths do not cross each other at any point.

Looking for Patterns

- It is recommended that children have completed the Inquisitive ant task, the Let's Investigate activity on page 1 and the previous Looking for Patterns activity before starting on this activity.
- Discuss with the children how to design their puzzle. Suggest that they start by writing in the multiples of 3 and 5 that form the two paths, and then write in the other numbers that are not multiples of 3 or 5. Also discuss what to do if the two paths cross each other (the number needs to be both a multiple of 3 and 5, e.g. 15, 30, 45, …).
- When children have completed their puzzle they swap with a friend and try and solve each other's puzzle.
- Suggest the children make a smaller puzzle than the 8 × 11 grid on the Resource sheet – perhaps a 6 × 6 grid.
- You may wish to begin this activity by discussing and writing down all the multiples of 3 and 5, and, if appropriate, those multiples that are common to both 3 and 5 (see comment above).

AfL

- How did you work out which two numbers when multiplied together made one of these numbers?
- Tell me a number that is both a multiple of three and a multiple of four. Can you tell me another number? These numbers are also multiples of what other numbers?
- Tell me a multiple of three / four / five. Tell me a number that is a multiple of three and five. What about a number that is a multiple of four and five?
- What would the final number be for a car with the number eight on it? What about the number ten?
- Can you use these number cards to make two three-digit numbers / one number which is twice the other number?
- How did you work out the answer to this problem / solution to this puzzle?
- Tell me some of the arrangements you made using these squares. What is this written as a multiplication number sentence?

Answers

Page 1

The Puzzler

17 × 2 = 34   16 × 3 = 48   13 × 4 = 52
14 × 6 = 84   18 × 5 = 90   15 × 8 = 120

Let's Investigate

Multiples of 3: 3, 6, 9, 12, 15, 18, 21, 24, 27, 30, 33, 36.
Multiples of 4: 4, 8, 12, 16, 20, 24, 28, 32, 36, 40, 44, 48.
Common multiples of 3 and 4: 12, 24 and 36.
The common multiples of 3 and 4 are all multiples of 12.
Multiples of 5: 5, 10, 15, 20, 25, 30, 35, 40, 45, 50, 55, 60.
Common multiples of 3 and 5: 15 and 30.

Page 2

Sports Update

car 1: 4
car 2: 20
car 3: 36
car 4: 52
car 5: 68
car 6: 84

Let's Investigate

Results of the investigation will vary.

Page 3

Let's Investigate

24 = 4 × 6 (or 6 × 4)
        1 × 24 (or 24 × 1), 2 × 12 (or 12 × 2), 3 × 8 (or 8 × 3)
Answers will vary but may include the following:
23 squares = 1 × 23
22 squares = 1 × 22, 2 × 11
21 squares = 1 × 21, 3 × 7
20 squares = 1 × 20, 2 × 10, 5 × 4
19 squares = 1 × 19
18 squares = 1 × 18, 2 × 9, 3 × 6
17 squares = 1 × 17
16 squares = 1 × 16, 2 × 8, 4 × 4
15 squares = 1 × 15, 3 × 5
14 squares = 1 × 14, 2 × 7
13 squares = 1 × 13
12 squares = 1 × 12, 2 × 6, 3 × 4
11 squares = 1 × 11
10 squares = 1 × 10, 2 × 5
9 squares = 1 × 9, 3 × 3
8 squares = 1 × 8, 2 × 4
7 squares = 1 × 7
6 squares = 1 × 6, 2 × 3
5 squares = 1 × 5
4 squares = 1 × 4, 2 × 2
3 squares = 1 × 3
2 squares = 1 × 2
1 square = 1 × 1

Money Matters

Cathy has £2, Madeline has £10, Coleen has £8, Jill has £4 and Peter has £6.

Page 4

Looking for Patterns

START	30	45	15	73	35	97	2	22	85
40	10	86	3	41	94	59	50	34	19
16	58	29	21	33	27	71	13	65	38
32	4	56	77	17	6	46	82	11	37
31	67	44	34	55	39	48	9	36	12
26	5	24	20	64	79	95	43	41	42
14	70	89	74	48	94	7	83	10	24
82	25	49	98	8	38	5	22	61	18
11	53	17	86	36	47	50	77	26	51
27	91	23	62	12	52	28	60	68	END

Looking for Patterns

Puzzles will vary.

Inquisitive ant

multiple
A number that can be divided exactly by another smaller number without a remainder.

Issue 10

Multiplication

Prerequisites for learning

- Recall and use multiplication and division facts for the 2, 5 and 10 multiplication tables
- Recognise multiples of 2, 5 and 10
- Count in steps of 3 and 4 from 0 and begin to count from 0 in other single-digit steps
- Understand that halving is the inverse of doubling and derive and recall doubles of all numbers to 20
- Use knowledge of number facts and operations to estimate and check answers to calculations
- Recall and use known multiplication facts to perform written and mental calculations
- Understand that division is the inverse of multiplication and vice versa; use this to derive and record related multiplication and division number sentences and to solve missing number problems
- Use the symbols × and = to record and interpret number sentences
- Use a calculator

Resources

pencil and paper

Resource sheet 2: My notes (optional)

Resource sheet 3: Pupil self assessment booklet (optional)

Resource sheet 6: 1 – 100 number squares

coloured pencils

calculator

Teaching support

Page 1

Looking for Patterns

- Children need to understand the term 'multiple' before starting on this activity and the 🏁 Looking for Patterns activity on page 2. Therefore, it is recommended that the children have completed Issue 9 – Multiplication, before starting either of these activities.
- There are two aspects to this activity. The first is to colour all the multiples of 2, 3, 4 and 5 on the four 1 – 100 number squares. The second, and more important aspect, is for the children to write about the patterns they notice in each of the four number squares.
- Once children have coloured all the multiples of 2, 3, 4 and 5 on the four 1 – 100 number squares, arrange them in pairs to compare and discuss their results. Children will need to have successfully completed this aspect of the activity before moving on to being able to identify any patterns. They also need to have completed the Resource sheet before starting on the 🏁 Looking for Patterns activity that follows.
- Encourage the children to write a statement to define the multiples of 2, 3, 4 and 5. For example, 'All multiples of 2 are even numbers. They end in 0, 2, 4, 6 or 8.' 'All multiples of 5 end in either 0 or 5.'

Looking for Patterns

- You may wish to suggest to the children that they write out the 2 multiplication table and the 4 multiplication table beside each other. This may help the children better identify the relationship between the two tables.

$$1 \times 2 = 2 \qquad \overset{\times 2}{\frown} \qquad 1 \times 4 = 4$$
$$2 \times 2 = 4 \qquad \overset{\times 2}{\frown} \qquad 2 \times 4 = 8$$
$$3 \times 2 = 6 \qquad \overset{\times 2}{\frown} \qquad 3 \times 4 = 12$$
$$4 \times 2 = 8 \qquad \overset{\times 2}{\frown} \qquad 4 \times 4 = 16$$
$$5 \times 2 = 10 \qquad \overset{\times 2}{\frown} \qquad 5 \times 4 = 20$$
$$6 \times 2 = 12 \qquad \overset{\times 2}{\frown} \qquad 6 \times 4 = 24$$
$$7 \times 2 = 14 \qquad \overset{\times 2}{\frown} \qquad 7 \times 4 = 28$$
$$8 \times 2 = 16 \qquad \overset{\times 2}{\frown} \qquad 8 \times 4 = 32$$
$$9 \times 2 = 18 \qquad \overset{\times 2}{\frown} \qquad 9 \times 4 = 36$$
$$10 \times 2 = 20 \qquad \overset{\times 2}{\frown} \qquad 10 \times 4 = 40$$

- Children investigate the statement: 'How does the 3 multiplication table help with the 6 multiplication table?'. If necessary, as above for the 2 and 4 multiplication tables, children should write out the 3 and 6 multiplication tables beside each other.

Page 2

Let's Investigate

- Tell the children that it is possible to make 16 different calculations using the 12 numbers and two symbols. Can they find them all?

- Encourage the children to be systematic in their recording of the different calculations they make.

Looking for Patterns

- Children need to have completed the first 🐜 Looking for Patterns activity on page 1 before starting on this activity. It is also recommended that they have completed Issue 9 – Multiplication.

- You may wish the children to work in pairs on this activity so that they can discuss their observations.

Page 3

Looking for Patterns

- Ensure the children are able to read and interpret the multiplication square. If this is something that is unfamiliar to the children you may need to spend some time discussing this with them.

- Children should be able to easily complete the 2, 5 and 10 multiplication tables rows and columns and possibly the 3 and 4 multiplication tables rows and columns. Ensure that the children realise that once these answers are on the grid there are only 16 multiplication tables facts remaining.

- Encourage the children to look continually for patterns in the rows and columns of the multiplication table. By being able to identify and continue these patterns they will be able to complete the table successfully.

Page 4

The Puzzler

- Some children may need assistance with the last two calculations.
- Some calculations have more than one possible answer. Can the children find them? (see Answers)

Technology Today

- Encourage the children to be systematic in their recording of the different calculations they make.

- Tell the children that it is possible to make nine different calculations using the three numbers and two symbols. Can they find them all? (see Answers)

AfL

- What patterns do you notice on this coloured 1 – 100 number square?
- How can the 2 multiplication table help you work out the answers to the 4 multiplication table? Is this the same for the 3 multiplication table helping you work out the answers to the 6 multiplication table?
- How many different number sentences were you able to make? What patterns / relationships do you notice between some of your number sentences? Can you use this pattern / relationship to tell me another number sentence you can make using these numbers?
- What patterns do you notice on this 100 square that has numbers coloured and circled?
- How did you work out the missing answers on this multiplication table chart? What patterns did you notice? How did these patterns help you?
- How did you know what digit to write in this box?
- What is the smallest / largest answer you can get on the calculator using just these keys?

Answers

Page 1

Looking for Patterns

1	2	3	4	5	6	7	8	9	10
11	12	13	14	15	16	17	18	19	20
21	22	23	24	25	26	27	28	29	30
31	32	33	34	35	36	37	38	39	40
41	42	43	44	45	46	47	48	49	50
51	52	53	54	55	56	57	58	59	60
61	62	63	64	65	66	67	68	69	70
71	72	73	74	75	76	77	78	79	80
81	82	83	84	85	86	87	88	89	90
91	92	93	94	95	96	97	98	99	100

Explanations will vary.

Looking for Patterns

The answers to the 4 multiplication table are double those of the 2 multiplication table.

Page 2

Let's Investigate

$2 \times 3 = 6$	$2 \times 10 = 20$	$3 \times 5 = 15$	$4 \times 15 = 60$
$2 \times 4 = 8$	$2 \times 15 = 30$	$3 \times 10 = 30$	$5 \times 6 = 30$
$2 \times 5 = 10$	$2 \times 30 = 60$	$3 \times 20 = 60$	$5 \times 12 = 60$
$2 \times 6 = 12$	$3 \times 4 = 12$	$4 \times 5 = 20$	$6 \times 10 = 60$

Page 3

Looking for Patterns

×	1	2	3	4	5	6	7	8	9	10
1	1	2	3	4	5	6	7	8	9	10
2	2	4	6	8	10	12	14	16	18	20
3	3	6	9	12	15	18	21	24	27	30
4	4	8	12	16	20	24	28	32	36	40
5	5	10	15	20	25	30	35	40	45	50
6	6	12	18	24	30	36	42	48	54	60
7	7	14	21	28	35	42	49	56	63	70
8	8	16	24	32	40	48	56	64	72	80
9	9	18	27	36	45	54	63	72	81	90
10	10	20	30	40	50	60	70	80	90	100

Page 4

The Puzzler

$\boxed{5} \times \boxed{2} = 10$ $1\boxed{5} \times \boxed{2} = 30$ $\boxed{5} \times 10 = \boxed{5}0$

or $\boxed{2} \times \boxed{5} = 10$ $\quad$ or $\boxed{2} \times 10 = \boxed{2}0$

$1\boxed{2} \times \boxed{5} = 60$ $1\boxed{5} \times 8 = 1\boxed{2}0$ $\boxed{2} \times 2\boxed{5} = \boxed{5}0$

Technology Today

$2 \times 3 = 6$	$23 \times 5 = 115$	$32 \times 5 = 160$	$52 \times 3 = 156$
$2 \times 5 = 10$	$25 \times 3 = 75$	$35 \times 2 = 70$	$53 \times 2 = 106$
$3 \times 5 = 15$			

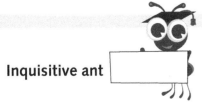

Inquisitive ant

common multiple

A number that can be divided exactly by two or more other numbers without a remainder. For example, 12 is a common multiple of 2, 3, 4 and 6.

Issue 11

Division

Prerequisites for learning

- Recall and use multiplication and division facts for the 2, 5 and 10 multiplication tables
- Recognise multiples of 2, 5 and 10
- Count in steps of 3 and 4 from 0 and begin to count from 0 in other single-digit steps
- Use knowledge of number facts and operations to estimate and check answers to calculations
- Represent repeated addition and arrays as multiplication, and sharing and repeated subtraction (grouping) as division
- Recall and use known multiplication and division facts to perform written and mental calculations
- Understand that division is the inverse of multiplication and vice versa; use this to derive and record related multiplication and division number sentences and to solve missing number problems
- Use the symbols ÷ and = to record and interpret number sentences

Resources

pencil and paper

Resource sheet 2: My notes (optional)

Resource sheet 3: Pupil self assessment booklet (optional)

Resource sheet 20: 2 cm squared paper

counters

set of 0 – 9 digit cards

calculator (optional)

Teaching support

Page 1

The Arts Roundup

- This activity involves the children recognising all the factors of 24.
- Provide the children with 24 counters (or similar) and ask them to find as many different ways as they can of arranging the counters into rectangles.
- If appropriate, introduce and discuss the word 'factor' with the children.

The Language of Maths

- Children's explanations will vary. However, they should realise that numbers that are divisible by 2 have 0, 2, 4, 6 or 8 in the ones place value and the numbers that are divisible by 5 have 0 or 5 in the ones place value. Therefore, a number divisible by both 2 and 5 must have a 0 in the ones place value because that is the only digit that is common to both groups. Any number that has a 0 in the ones place value is divisible by 10.
- If appropriate, introduce and discuss the word 'divisible' with the children.
- Children investigate the statement, 'If a number can be divided by 2 and by 3, then it can also be divided by 6'.

Page 2

The Puzzler

- Some children may need assistance with the last two calculations.
- The first calculation has more than one possible answer. Can the children find them both?

Let's Investigate

- Explain to the children how each array must include more than one row or column of counters. For example:

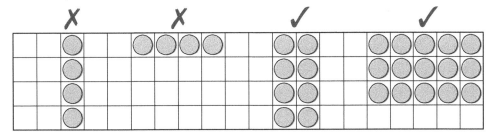

- Discuss with the children the link between multiplication and division, i.e.

    $10 \div 5 = 2$

    $10 \div 2 = 5$

    $2 \times 5 = 10$

    $5 \times 2 = 10$

- Ask the children to write down those calculations that make squares. What do they know about these numbers?

- Children use more than 30 counters.

Page 3

Let's Investigate

- Prior to the children working independently on this activity, ensure that they fully understand the investigation.
- Also ensure that the children make an estimation of how many times they think they will complete their name on the paving stones.

- What if there were 22 paving stones? What about 27 paving stones?

The Puzzler

- If necessary, remind the children of those numbers that are divisible by 5, i.e. 5, 10, 15, 20, …

Page 4

Let's Investigate

- This activity introduces children to the test of divisibility for multiples of 3, i.e. the sum of the digits is divisible by 3.
- Ask the children to investigate whether the same rule applies for three-digit and four-digit numbers. They can check their reasoning using a calculator.

Let's Investigate

- Children can simply use the cards to make different multiples of 3 and 4. An alternative, and more challenging task, is to ask the children to make different groups of numbers that are multiples of 3 or 4 using each of the digits 0 – 9 once only in each group of numbers (as in the example in the issue). For example:

- Encourage the children to make combinations of two-digit and three-digit numbers.

AfL

- How did you work out the answer to this problem / solution to this puzzle?
- So is Michael's statement always true, sometimes true or never true? Why do you say that?
- How did you work out what digit to write in this box?
- Can you describe this array for me as a multiplication number sentence? Is there another multiplication number sentence that describes this array?
- Were you able to write your name several times on these stones without having to leave out any letters? Why was this?
- How did you work out the solution to this puzzle?
- How do you know that a number can be divided exactly by three? Can the number 123 be divided exactly by three? What about the number 342 / 104 / 111?
- Tell me some numbers that can be divided by three / four.

Answers

Page 1

The Arts Roundup
Groups of 24, 12, 8, 6, 4, 3 and 2.

The Language of Maths
Michael's statement is always true.
Explanations will vary.

Page 2

The Puzzler
8 ÷ 2 = 4   2 0 ÷ 5 = 4   2 00 ÷ 4 = 50
or 8 ÷ 4 = 2
4 0 ÷ 2 = 2 0   4 8 ÷ 4 = 1 2   2 4 ÷ 2 = 1 2

Let's Investigate
Rectangles and calculations will vary.

Page 3

Let's Investigate
Results of the investigation will vary.
Anyone's name containing a number of letters that is a factor
of 20 would be able to write their name over and over again
fitting exactly the number of stones.

The Puzzler

8	3	✗	9
4	2	1	3
2	✗	7	6
1	5	7	2

Page 4

Let's Investigate
Results of the investigation will vary.

Let's Investigate
Results of the investigation will vary.

Inquisitive ant

divisible
A number is divisible by another number if it can be divided exactly by
that number without a remainder.

Issue 12

Division

Prerequisites for learning

- Recall and use multiplication and division facts for the 2, 5 and 10 multiplication tables
- Recognise multiples of 2, 5 and 10
- Count in steps of 3 and 4 from 0 and begin to count from 0 in other single-digit steps
- Use knowledge of number facts and operations to estimate and check answers to calculations
- Represent repeated addition and arrays as multiplication, and sharing and repeated subtraction (grouping) as division
- Recall and use known multiplication and division facts to perform written and mental calculations
- Understand that division is the inverse of multiplication and vice versa; use this to derive and record related multiplication and division number sentences and to solve missing number problems
- Use the symbols ÷ and = to record and interpret number sentences

Resources

pencil and paper
Resource sheet 2: My notes (optional)
Resource sheet 3: Pupil self assessment booklet (optional)
counters
2 × 1 – 6 dice
interlocking cubes
pot / container

Teaching support

Page 1

What's the Problem?

- Provide the children with 36 counters (or similar) to represent the eggs.

The Puzzler

- Some children may need assistance with recording their working out. Encourage the children not to draw elaborate trains but just boxes as a simple system of recording. For example:

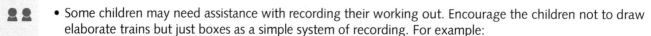

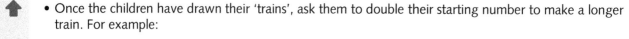

- Once the children have drawn their 'trains', ask them to double their starting number to make a longer train. For example:

  56 ← 28 → 14 → 7

  80 ← 40 → 20 → 10 → 5

- Children start with a three-digit number.

Page 2

Let's Investigate

- It is recommended that the children complete the Inquisitive Ant task before starting on this activity.
- Once the children have completed the activity, discuss with them the patterns they noticed and how this helped them to identify other numbers that when divided by 10 have a remainder of 2, 3 or 7, or that when divided by 5 have a remainder of 1, 2, 3 or 4.
- If appropriate, discuss with the children how to write a division calculation involving remainders, e.g. 42 ÷ 10 = 4 r 2; 82 ÷ 10 = 8 r 2.

The Puzzler

- Once the children have completed the activity, as a group discuss the various mental calculation strategies children used to estimate which number on a cake when divided by a number on a plate gives a number on a present.

- If necessary, discuss with the children the inverse relationship between multiplication and division. Can they use this relationship to identify a number on a plate that when multiplied by a number on a present has an answer that is one of the numbers on the cakes? For example, $6 \times 11 = 66$, so $66 \div 6 = 11$.

- If necessary, tell the children one of the pairs of numbers and the quotient (see Answers).

Page 3

The Puzzler

- Although this activity involves multiplication, it is designed to help the children see the link between multiplication and division, and the multiples of 2, 3, 4, 5 and 6 (up to the 6th multiple). Ensure that the children are familiar with the term 'multiple' before they work on this activity.
- Children need to have an understanding of the 2, 3, 4 and 5 multiplication tables for this activity. If they have, then the only multiplication table fact that the children may have some difficulty with is 6×6.
- Do the children realise that if, for example, they roll a 3 and a 4, then the product, i.e. 12, can be written in both these boxes (as well as in the multiple of 2 box)?
- Children should be able to write three numbers in each box before they write two numbers in the waste bin, because, in actual fact there is only one number that belongs in the waste bin, i.e. 1. All the other products possible are multiples of 2, 3, 4, 5 or 10.

Page 4

Let's Investigate

- Ensure that the children realise that they play the game by themselves. It is not until the second part of this activity, when children think about how to convert the activity into a game, that they work in pairs.

- Some children may not be as familiar with the 3 and 4 multiplication tables. If necessary, work with them to recall these facts, if necessary writing the answers beside the fact on the grid.

AfL

- How did you work out the answer to this problem / solution to this puzzle?
- What was the longest train you could make?
- Tell me some numbers that have a remainder of 1 when divided by 4 / 3?
- How did you work out which number divided by another number gives the answer to one of the numbers on the presents?
- Which numbers did you write on the waste bin? Why was there only one number?
- Which numbers did you write on 2 / 3 / 4 boxes?

Answers

Page 1

What's the Problem?
1 friend gets 36 eggs.
2 friends get 18 eggs each.
3 friends get 12 eggs each.
4 friends get 9 eggs each.
6 friends get 6 eggs each.
9 friends get 4 eggs each.
12 friends get 3 eggs each.
18 friends get 2 eggs each.
36 friends get 1 egg each.

The Puzzler
Three-carriage trains may include:
4, 2, 1
12, 6, 3
20, 10, 5, …
Four-carriage trains may include:
8, 4, 2, 1
24, 12, 6, 3
40, 20, 10, 5, …
Five-carriage trains may include:
16, 8, 4, 2, 1
48, 24, 12, 6, 3
80, 40, 20, 10, 5, …
The largest train that can be made starting with a two-digit
number is a seven-carriage train: 64, 32, 16, 8, 4, 2, 1.

Page 2

Let's Investigate
Numbers that have a remainder of 3 when divided by 10 may
include: 13, 23, 33, 43, 53, …
Numbers that have a remainder of 7 when divided by 10 may
include: 17, 27, 37, 47, 57, …
Numbers that have a remainder of 1 when divided by 5 may
include: 6, 11, 16, 21, 26, …
Numbers that have a remainder of 2 when divided by 5 may
include: 7, 12, 17, 22, 27, …
Numbers that have a remainder of 3 when divided by 5 may
include: 8, 13, 18, 23, 28, …
Numbers that have a remainder of 4 when divided by 5 may
include: 9, 14, 19, 24, 29, …

The Puzzler
$66 \div 6 = 11$ $96 \div 8 = 12$ $52 \div 4 = 13$
$28 \div 2 = 14$ $45 \div 3 = 15$ $80 \div 5 = 16$

Page 3

The Puzzler
Numbers will vary.

Page 4

Let's Investigate
No answer required.

Inquisitive ant

remainder
The amount left over when a number or quantity cannot be divided
exactly by another number.

Issue 13

Mixed operations

Prerequisites for learning

- Describe patterns and relationships involving numbers
- Recall and use addition and subtraction facts to 20 fluently, and derive and use related facts up to 100
- Understand that halving is the inverse of doubling and derive and recall doubles of all numbers to at least 20, and the corresponding halves
- Recall and use multiplication and division facts for the 2, 5 and 10 multiplication tables
- Use knowledge of number facts and operations to estimate and check answers to calculations
- Add more than two numbers
- Understand that subtraction is the inverse of addition and vice versa; use this to derive and record related addition and subtraction number sentences and to solve missing number problems
- Use the symbols +, −, ×, ÷ and = to record and interpret number sentences
- Begin to understand the order of operations

Resources

pencil and paper
Resource sheet 2: My notes (optional)
Resource sheet 3: Pupil self assessment booklet (optional)
calculator (optional)
two different coloured counters, or similar (optional)
computer with internet access (optional)

Teaching support

Page 1

Looking for Patterns

- Allow the children to use a calculator.
- Can the children explain, using numbers or symbols, how each of these puzzles work? For example:

Think of a number.	○
Add 4.	○ + 4
Multiply this answer by 2.	○○ + 8
Subtract 6.	○○ + 2
Halve this answer.	○ + 1
Subtract the number you first thought of.	1
Think of a number.	△
Multiply by 5.	△△△△△
Add 2.	△△△△△ + 2
Double this answer.	△△△△△△△△△△ + 4
Subtract 4.	△△△△△△△△△△
Divide this number by 10.	△

The Puzzler

- Before the children go off to work independently on the puzzle, ensure that they understand how the addition table works.
- Once the children have completed the table, discuss with them their methods for working out the missing numbers. If appropriate, discuss with them the inverse relationship between addition and subtraction.

Page 2

The Language of Maths

- Before the children go off to work independently on this activity, discuss with them some of the possible contexts they might use to describe their class. For example, children sitting at particular tables, boys and girls, clothing, … . Encourage the children to be as imaginative in their contexts as possible.

- You may need to remind children to write down their statements.

- Where appropriate, encourage the children to use fractions to describe the class.

- Once individuals or pairs of children have written down several statements, ask them to look at all their statements and decide which is their favourite. Then hold a group discussion where children share their statements, and in particular their favourite. Ask the children to say why they consider a particular statement is their favourite.

Let's Investigate

- Ensure the children are able to read and interpret the grids. If appropriate, draw their attention to the similarities of the grids in this activity and the grid in 🐜 The Puzzler activity on page 1.

- Ask the children to copy each of the grids and inside each area write one (or two) true statements. For example:

+	ODD	EVEN
ODD	5 + 7 = 12	9 + 6 = 15
EVEN	4 + 5 = 9	6 + 8 = 14

Page 3

Construct

- The children will get more out of this activity if, before they go off to work independently, there is a group discussion about what type of machine they would invent, why they would invent it, and the components they would need to make it.

- The open-ended nature of this activity means that children can be as precise and accurate as both you and they want, especially with respect to assigning a value to the different parts of the machine and working out the machine's total cost.

- If appropriate, allow the children to use the internet to help them cost the various parts of their machine, and also a calculator to work out the total cost.

Money Matters

- Suggest the children draw a table to work out the answers to the three questions, e.g.

Alice	Michael
£2	£3
£4	£6
£6	£9
£8	£12
£10	£15
£12	£18

- Provide the children with two different-coloured counters (or similar) to represent £2 and £3.

Page 4

Let's Investigate

- You may need to discuss with the children how a number sentence can involve more than three numbers and one operation.

- Ask the children if they can find more than one way of arranging the digits 1 – 8 and the four operations to make two number sentences (see Answers).

- If appropriate, discuss with the children the order of operations.

What's the Problem?

- Discuss with the children the number of legs on one chicken (i.e. 2) and one goat (i.e. 4).
- Suggest the children draw a simple diagram, and use trial and improvement, to help them work out the solution, for example:

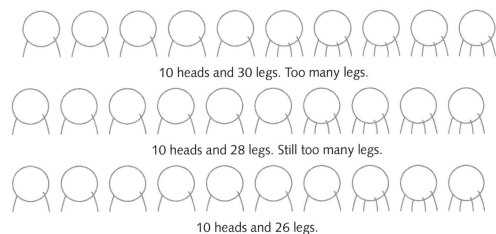

10 heads and 30 legs. Too many legs.

10 heads and 28 legs. Still too many legs.

10 heads and 26 legs.

So that's 7 chickens and 3 goats.

AfL

- What was your final answer in this puzzle? What did you notice about this number? Was it the same for any number you started with?
- How did you work out the missing numbers in this puzzle?
- Tell me one of the statements you wrote about your class.
- What can you tell me about the sum of / difference between an odd and even number? What about two even / two odd numbers? Give me an example.
- What happens when you multiply an odd number by an even number? What about when you multiply two even / odd numbers together?
- How much is your machine worth? Tell me how you got to that amount.
- How did you work out the answer to this problem / solution to this puzzle?
- How else did you arrange the digits and the four symbols to make two number sentences? Could you make two different number sentences for me?

Answers

Page 1

Looking for Patterns
The final answer is always 1.
The final answer is always the number you first thought of.

The Puzzler

+	6	2	9	3
7	13	**9**	**16**	10
4	**10**	6	13	**7**
8	14	**10**	17	**11**
10	16	12	**19**	13

Page 2

The Language of Maths
Sentences will vary.

Let's Investigate

+	ODD	EVEN
ODD	EVEN	ODD
EVEN	ODD	EVEN

–	ODD	EVEN
ODD	EVEN	ODD
EVEN	ODD	EVEN

×	ODD	EVEN
ODD	ODD	EVEN
EVEN	EVEN	EVEN

Page 3

Construct
Designs and costs will vary.

Money Matters
Michael has saved £12.
Alice has saved £6.
Michael has saved £18 and Alice has saved £12.

Page 4

Let's Investigate
Other possible calculations include:

$8 \times 1 - 3 = 5$ $6 \div 2 + 4 = 7$
$8 - 7 + 4 = 5$ $6 \div 2 \times 1 = 3$
$4 \times 3 - 5 = 7$ $2 \div 1 + 6 = 8$
$6 \times 2 - 5 = 7$ $8 \div 4 + 1 = 3$

What's the Problem?
There are 7 chickens and 3 goats on the farm.

Inquisitive ant

operator
The mathematical symbol in a calculation that describes the operation, i.e. +, –, × and ÷.

Mixed operations

Prerequisites for learning

- Describe patterns and relationships involving numbers
- Recall and use addition and subtraction facts to 20 fluently, and derive and use related facts up to 100
- Recall and use multiplication and division facts for the 2, 5 and 10 multiplication tables
- Recognise multiples of 2, 5 and 10
- Use knowledge of number facts and operations to estimate and check answers to calculations
- Add and subtract numbers using concrete objects, pictorial representations, and mentally, including:
  - a two-digit number and ones
  - a two-digit number and tens
  - two two-digit numbers
  - adding three one-digit numbers
- Understand that subtraction is the inverse of addition and vice versa; use this to derive and record related addition and subtraction number sentences and to solve missing number problems
- Understand that division is the inverse of multiplication and vice versa; use this to derive and record related multiplication and division number sentences and to solve missing number problems
- Use the symbols +, −, ×, ÷ and = to record and interpret number sentences
- Begin to understand the order of operations

Resources

pencil and paper

Resource sheet 2: My notes (optional)

Resource sheet 3: Pupil self assessment booklet (optional)

5p, 10p, 20p, 50p, £1, £2 coins (optional)

calculator (optional)

Teaching support

Page 1

Money Matters

- Assist the children in starting the problem by giving them one or two examples:

  Child 1: £1   Child 1: £1 + 50p + 10p

  Child 2: 50p + 20p   Child 2: 20p + 20p

  Child 3: 20p + 20p + 20p + 20p   Child 3: 50p

- Encourage the children to come up with as many different combinations of coins as possible.
- Provide the children with a selection of 5p, 10p, 20p, 50p, £1 and £2 coins.
- As well as no two children having the same amount of money or the same number of coins, what if they also didn't have any of the same coins as another child? What coins might each child have?

Let's Investigate

- Ask the children to look for two / three different solutions for each number sentence.
- Once the children have completed the activity, arrange them into pairs or groups and ask the children to share the different solutions they found for each of the number sentences.

Page 2

The Puzzler

• Ensure the children can read and interpret the shapes. If necessary, work through the first shape with the children.

Page 3

The Arts Roundup

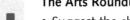

• Suggest the children use trial and improvement to work out the number of men and women in the choir.

Also remind the children that the two numbers must total 28 and have a difference of 6.

Let's Investigate

• This activity is designed to practise and consolidate children's known multiplication tables facts. Children will get more out of this activity if they have some understanding of the multiplication facts other than just the 2, 5 and 10 multiplication tables. However, just knowing these facts, children can successfully complete the activity (see Answers).

• This activity also introduces children to calculations involving more than one operation. Ensure the children understand the two examples in the issue. If appropriate, discuss with the children the convention of using brackets.

• Once children have completed the activity, arrange them into pairs to compare and discuss their results.

• Encourage the children to use multiplication facts other than the 2, 5 and 10 multiplication tables.

• Ask the children to find more than one way of making each of the multiples of 10, e.g.

$(2 \times 2) + (2 \times 3)$ $(2 \times 4) + (2 \times 1)$

$= 4 + 6$ $= 8 + 2$

$= 10$ $= 10$

• Can the children use subtraction to work out the multiples of 10, e.g.

$(2 \times 10) - (2 \times 5)$ $(4 \times 10) - (2 \times 10)$

$= 20 - 10$ $= 40 - 20$

$= 10$ $= 20$

Page 4

Let's Investigate

• This activity introduces children to the concept of 'trios', i.e. different sets of three numbers that can be used to make two addition and two subtraction calculations, or two multiplication and two division calculations.

• The activity also consolidates the inverse relationships between addition and subtraction, and multiplication and division; and the commutative law as it applies to addition and multiplication.

• Once children have written sufficient trios, arrange them into pairs to compare and discuss their results.

Money Matters

• Ensure the children realise that the different notes that Colin could have in his wallet are £5, £10 and £20.

• There are two possible solutions to this problem, ask the children to find both of them.

AfL

- What coins might the children have had? Could they have had different coins? What might they have been?
- What number did you write in these boxes to complete this number sentence? What other numbers could you have written in these boxes?
- Tell me the calculations you did to work out how many were going to St Ives.
- How did you solve this problem / puzzle? What calculations did you do?
- What is the value of this part of the shape? What is the total value of the shape? How did you work that out?
- What multiplication facts did you use to give an answer of 80 / 100? Could you have used different multiplication tables?
- Tell me three numbers that give two addition and two subtraction number sentences. How are these number sentences related?
- Tell me three numbers that give two multiplication and two division number sentences. What is the relationship between these four number sentences?

Answers

Page 1

Money Matters
Amounts will vary.

Let's Investigate
Calculations will vary.

Page 2

The Puzzler

A =	12	A =	5	A =	2	A =	6	A =	4
B =	8	B =	10	B =	5	B =	12	B =	4
C =	8	C =	15	C =	8	C =	3	C =	16
Total =	32	Total =	40	Total =	16	Total =	27	Total =	32

Page 3

The Arts Roundup
There are 11 men and 17 women in the choir.

Let's Investigate
Solutions will vary but may involve calculations similar to the following:

(5 × 4) + (2 × 5)	(5 × 4) + (2 × 10)
= 20 + 10	= 20 + 20
= 30	= 40
(2 × 10) + (3 × 10)	(4 × 10) + (2 × 10)
= 20 + 30	= 40 + 20
= 50	= 60
(4 × 10) + (3 × 10)	(6 × 10) + (2 × 10)
= 40 + 30	= 60 + 20
= 70	= 80
(5 × 10) + (4 × 10)	(6 × 10) + (4 × 10)
= 50 + 40	= 60 + 40
= 90	= 100

Page 4

Let's Investigate
Trios will vary.

Money Matters
Two solutions are possible:
(1 × £20) + (5 × £10) + (1 × £5)
(2 × £20) + (2 × £10) + (3 × £5)

Inquisitive ant  value

1. The numeral quantity given to a mathematical symbol.

2. The material or monetary worth of something.

Issue 15

Mixed operations

Prerequisites for learning

- Describe patterns and relationships involving numbers
- Recall and use addition and subtraction facts to 20 fluently, and derive and use related facts up to 100
- Recall and use multiplication and division facts for the 2, 5 and 10 multiplication tables
- Recognise multiples of 2, 5 and 10
- Use knowledge of number facts and operations to estimate and check answers to calculations
- Add and subtract numbers using concrete objects, pictorial representations, and mentally, including:
  - a two-digit number and ones
  - a two-digit number and tens
  - two two-digit numbers
  - adding three one-digit numbers
- Recall and use known multiplication and division facts to perform written and mental calculations
- Understand that subtraction is the inverse of addition and vice versa; use this to derive and record related addition and subtraction number sentences and to solve missing number problems
- Understand that division is the inverse of multiplication and vice versa; use this to derive and record related multiplication and division number sentences and to solve missing number problems
- Use the symbols +, −, ×, ÷ and = to record and interpret number sentences
- Use a calculator

Resources

pencil and paper

Resource sheet 2: My notes (optional)

Resource sheet 3: Pupil self assessment booklet (optional)

20 × £1 coins or counters (optional)

calculator

Teaching support

Page 1

The Puzzler

- Tell the children what the total is for the first puzzle. (15)
- Tell the children that there is more than one solution for each puzzle. Can they find several?

Money Matters

- From the clues, it is possible to order the friends according to how much money they have – Fabio has the least amount, then Justin and Louise. Sarah has the most money. Once the children know this, they can then use the clues, and trial and improvement, to work out how much money each friend has.
- If necessary, allow the children to use 20 × £1 coins or counters. They can then use the clues to divide the coins / counters between four to see how much money each friend has.

Page 2

Looking for Patterns

- In any 3 × 3, 5 × 5, 7 × 7 or 9 × 9 square the total of both pairs of diagonally opposite numbers is always twice the number in the middle of the square. The total of pairs of numbers symmetrically opposite the middle number also give the same total, e.g.

31	32	33
41	(42)	43
51	52	53

56	57	58	59	60
66	67	68	69	70
76	77	(78)	79	80
86	87	88	89	90
96	97	98	99	100

31 + 53 = 84
33 + 51 = 84

42 × 2 = 84

32 + 52 = 84
41 + 43 = 84

56 + 100 = 156
60 + 96 = 156

78 × 2 = 156

57 + 99 = 156
58 + 98 = 156
59 + 97 = 156
66 + 90 = 156
67 + 89 = 156

68 + 88 = 156
69 + 87 = 156
70 + 86 = 156
76 + 80 = 156
77 + 79 = 156

- In 4 × 4, 6 × 6 and 8 × 8 squares there is no middle number, although the total of pairs of numbers symmetrically opposite do give the same total, e.g.

6	7	8	9
16	17	18	19
26	27	28	29
36	37	38	39

6 + 39 = 45
9 + 36 = 45

7 + 38 = 45
8 + 37 = 45
16 + 29 = 45
17 + 28 = 45
18 + 27 = 45
19 + 26 = 45

What's the Problem?

- Before working independently on this activity ensure the children understand that in a division situation a remainder (or an amount left over) can occur after an equal sharing or grouping has been completed.
- Suggest the children make lists to help them identify Miss Walker's age, e.g.

I am more than twenty, but less than thirty.

21, 22, 23, 24, 25, 26, 27, 28, 29

If you divide my age by two you are left with 1.

21, 23, 25, 27, 29

If you divide my age by three you are left with 2.

23, 26, 29

If you divide my age by five you are left with 4.

24, 29

Only one number matches all four clues, i.e. 29.

Page 3

The Language of Maths

- Some children may need help in writing their own secret message using the letters given. If this is the case, suggest they write several words instead or write some other calculations with an accompanying letter, in order to give them more letters to use, for example, 20 – 7 = ☐ ⇨ A. However, ensure the children realise that they cannot write a calculation where the answer is the same number as one of the calculations in the issue.

Page 4

What's the Problem?

- Ensure children realise that emus have two legs and llamas have four legs.
- Suggest the children draw a simple diagram, and use trial and improvement, to help them work out the solution. Also remind the children that Farmer Giles has one more llama than he has emus.

Technology Today

- The main focus of this activity is the strategies that children develop as they play the games in order to help them win. Therefore, once pairs of children have played the game several times, arrange the pairs into groups and discuss with the children the various strategies they used to help them win the game.
- Children take turns entering 1, 2, 3, 4 or 5. The player whose turn ends on 41 is the winner.

AfL

- What strategies did you use to help you work out the answer to this problem / solution to this puzzle?
- How else might you have worked it out?
- What patterns are there in the numbers that are diagonally opposite each other in a 2 × 2 square on a 1 – 100 number square?
  What about in a 3 × 3 / 4 × 4 / 5 × 5 square?
- Did you notice any other patterns in the smaller squares on a 1 – 100 number square?
- What were some good strategies that helped you win the game? Did they always work? Why not?

Answers

Page 1

The Puzzler

9	5	1
2	7	6
4	3	8

	1	10	
9	2	7	8
3	12	5	6
	11	4	

Other solutions are possible.

Money Matters
Fabio £3
Justin £4
Louise £6
Sarah £7

Page 2

Looking for Patterns
The sum of pairs of diagonally opposite numbers in any square within a 1 – 100 number square is always the same.

What's the Problem?
Miss Walker is 29 years old.

Page 3

The Language of Maths

25 + 7 = 32	**O**	15 + 21 = 36 **N**
42 – 33 = 9	**H**	5 × 3 = 15 **C**
80 ÷ 2 = 40	**R**	21 ÷ 3 = 7 **B**
24 ÷ 2 = 12	**E**	15 – 7 = 8 **T**
8 × 3 = 24	**I**	35 – 17 = 18 **F**
2 × 5 = 10	**S**	100 ÷ 4 = 25 **L**

The secret file is in the office.

Page 4

What's the Problem?
Farmer Giles has four emus and five llamas.

Technology Today
Strategies will vary.

Inquisitive ant

calculator
A small hand-held instrument used to perform arithmetic calculations.

Issue 16

Mixed operations

Prerequisites for learning

- Describe patterns and relationships involving numbers
- Derive and recall doubles of all numbers to 20, and the corresponding halves
- Recall and use addition and subtraction facts to 20 fluently, and derive and use related facts up to 100
- Recall and use multiplication and division facts for the 2, 5 and 10 multiplication tables
- Recognise multiples of 2, 5 and 10
- Use knowledge of number facts and operations to estimate and check answers to calculations
- Add and subtract numbers using concrete objects, pictorial representations, and mentally, including:
  - a two-digit number and ones
  - a two-digit number and tens
  - two two-digit numbers
  - adding three one-digit numbers
- Recall and use known multiplication and division facts to perform written and mental calculations
- Understand that subtraction is the inverse of addition and vice versa; use this to derive and record related addition and subtraction number sentences and to solve missing number problems
- Understand that division is the inverse of multiplication and vice versa; use this to derive and record related multiplication and division number sentences and to solve missing number problems
- Use the symbols +, −, ×, ÷ and = to record and interpret number sentences

Resources

pencil and paper

Resource sheet 2: My notes (optional)

Resource sheet 3: Pupil self assessment booklet (optional)

counters, or similar (optional) in two colours

Teaching support

Page 1

Money Matters

- Suggest the children use trial and improvement to work out the number of apples and oranges Sally bought. Also remind the children that Sally bought twice as many oranges as apples and that she spent a total of £3.

- Suggest the children draw a diagram, adding two oranges for every one apple, and keeping a running total as they go, e.g.

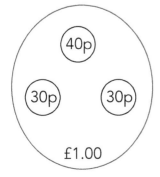

£1.00

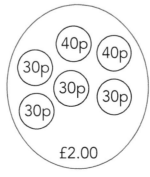

£2.00

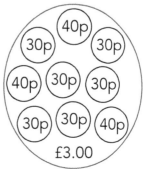

£3.00

The Puzzler

- Suggest the children use trial and improvement, e.g.

  If you add 18 to me, you get the same answer as multiplying me by 10.

Trial number	+ 18	× 10
5	23	50
3	21	30
2	20	20

✗ Number too big
✗ Number too big
✓

- Children write similar problems of their own for a friend to solve.

Page 2

Let's Investigate

- Some children may need assistance in setting out and organising their work. Suggest they present their work in columns as shown in the issue.
- Ask the children to investigate using two-digit numbers greater than 20.

Page 3

Looking for Patterns

- Remind the children that, at first, they are not expected to work out the actual answer to each of the six calculations, only make an estimation.
- Once the children have completed the activity, arrange them into pairs or groups and discuss and compare the various strategies they used to estimate and calculate the answers to each of the calculations.

What's the Problem?

- This activity involves division as grouping, and also informally introduces the children to the concept of ratio.
- Suggest the children draw a diagram to help them work out the solution to this problem.

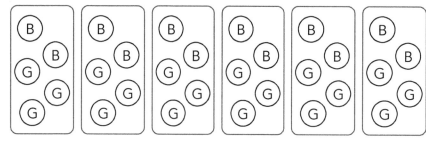

- If necessary, provide the children with counters (or similar) in two different colours: one colour to represent the boys, the other colour to represent the girls.

Page 4

Money Matters

- Ensure children realise that the price of a pie is on the blackboard menu.
- Suggest the children use trial and improvement, substituting prices for the burger and kebab. You may also wish to suggest to the children that they work out the price of a kebab first.

Technology Today

- Suggest the children draw a diagram to find out how many friends went on the picnic, e.g.

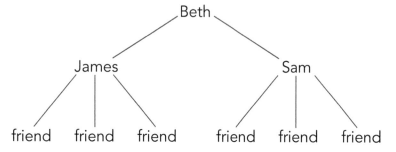

• What if all the friends that James and Sam invited each invited another two friends to go on the picnic? How many people would that be altogether? (21)

• What patterns do you notice? Why do you think this happens?
• How did you solve this problem / puzzle? How do you know that your answer is correct? How could you check your answer?
• How else could you work out the answer to this problem / solution to this puzzle?
• What did you think about when you approximated the answer to this calculation?

Answers

Page 1

Money Matters
Sally bought 3 apples and 6 oranges.

The Puzzler
2
12
1

Page 2

Let's Investigate
Numbers that end in 1:
1 (3 steps); 2 (1 step); 4 (2 steps); 5 (4 steps); 7 (6 steps); 8 (3 steps); 10 (5 steps); 11 (8 steps); 13 (5 steps); 14 (7 steps); 16 (4 steps); 17 (7 steps); 19 (10 steps); 20 (6 steps).

Numbers that repeat themselves:
3 (after 1 step); 6 (after 1 step); 9 (after 3 steps); 12 (after 2 steps); 15 (after 5 steps); 18 (after 4 steps).

Explanations of patterns will vary. However, children should notice that the numbers that repeat themselves are all multiples of 3.

Page 3

Looking for Patterns
$28 + 58 \approx 90$ (= 86)
$86 - 47 \approx 40$ (= 39)
$12 \times 6 \approx 70$ (= 72)
$58 \div 2 \approx 30$ (= 29)
$63 \div 3 \approx 20$ (= 21)
$23 + 14 + 16 \approx 50$ (= 53)

What's the Problem?
There are 18 girls and 12 boys in Mrs Rose's class.

Page 4

Money Matters
Burger = £5
Kebab = £4

Technology Today
9 friends went for a picnic.
Explanations will vary.

Inquisitive ant  estimation
A rough calculation of the value, number or quantity.

Mixed operations

Prerequisites for learning

- Describe patterns and relationships involving numbers
- Derive and recall doubles of all numbers to 20
- Recall and use addition and subtraction facts to 20 fluently, and derive and use related facts up to 100
- Recall and use multiplication and division facts for the 2, 5 and 10 multiplication tables
- Use knowledge of number facts and operations to estimate and check answers to calculations
- Add and subtract numbers using concrete objects, pictorial representations, and mentally, including:
  - a two-digit number and ones
  - a two-digit number and tens
  - two two-digit numbers
  - adding three one-digit numbers
- Recall and use known multiplication and division facts to perform written and mental calculations
- Understand that subtraction is the inverse of addition and vice versa; use this to derive and record related addition and subtraction number sentences and to solve missing number problems
- Understand that division is the inverse of multiplication and vice versa; use this to derive and record related multiplication and division number sentences and to solve missing number problems
- Use the symbols +, −, ×, ÷ and = to record and interpret number sentences

Resources

pencil and paper

Resource sheet 2: My notes (optional)

Resource sheet 3: Pupil self assessment booklet (optional)

Resource sheet 8: Number sentences

scissors

selection of coins, real or play (optional)

counters

several different mobile phones (optional)

Teaching support

Page 1

The Puzzler

- You may want to ensure that the answers to the children's four calculations are correct before they give their cards to a friend.
- There are two aspects to this activity. The first is writing four calculations; the second is arranging a friend's cards to make four calculations. The second part of this activity is harder than some children may at first think.

- Tell the children to write just addition and subtraction or multiplication and division calculations.
- Ask the children to write three, rather than four, calculations.
- Encourage the children to use fractions in one of their calculations for example, $\frac{1}{2}$ of 16 or $\frac{1}{4}$ of 12.

Page 2

Let's Investigate
- Finding solutions to numbers 18 and 28 are the two that children may have most difficulty with.
- Once children have completed the activity, arrange them in pairs to compare and discuss their calculations.

- For some of the numbers it is possible to make more than one calculation. Ask the children to find these.
- If appropriate, discuss with the children the convention of using brackets.

Technology Today

- Suggest the children draw a table or picture to work out how much Habiba has spent on mobile phone calls, and how many free texts she gets e.g.

Money spent	£10	£20	£30	£40	£50	£60	£70	£80
Free texts	50	100	150	200	250	300	350	400

Page 3

Money Matters

- Encourage the children to be systematic in their recording of the different possible combinations of coins.
- Provide the children with a selection of 1p, 2p, 5p and 10p coins.

Let's Investigate

- Do the children realise that while it is possible to make many different calculations, there are only four different totals possible: 27, 28, 29, and 30? If appropriate, discuss with the children why this is.
- When arranging the digits 1 to 9 on the other two hop-scotch grids to make the largest and smallest possible totals, ensure that the children realise that there are many different possible arrangements of the digits.

Page 4

Technology Today

- Children investigate whether or not they get the same totals for all mobile phones. What about landline phones? They could either do this in school by having a brief look at some of the mobile phones that adults working in the school use, or alternatively they could find this out at home.

The Puzzler

- While most children should find the first five questions relatively easy, some children may need assistance with the last three questions that involve more than one operation.
- Once the children have completed the activity, arrange them in pairs or groups and discuss how they knew which operation belonged in each of the circles.

AfL

- How did you work out the answer to this problem / solution to this puzzle?
- What patterns did you notice?
- Was your puzzle easy or hard? Why was it so easy? What made it so hard?
- Which numbers were easy to make using the darts? Which numbers did you really have to think about? Why?
- What are the different totals you could make? How did you make the largest / smallest total?
- What patterns did you notice when adding the keys on a mobile phone? Are the totals the same for all phones? Why is this?
- How did you know that the missing sign had to be a multiplication / division sign?

Answers

Page 1

The Puzzler
Number sentences will vary.

Page 2

Let's Investigate
Answers will vary.
Possible answers may include:

1 = 1	2 = 2
3 = 2 + 1	4 = (2 × 2)
5 = 5	6 = 5 + 1
7 = 5 + 2	8 = 5 + 2 + 1
9 = (2 × 2) + 5	10 = 10
11 = 10 +1	12 = 10 + 2
13 = 10 + 2 + 1	14 = 10 + (2 × 2)
15 = 10 + 5	16 = 10 + 5 + 1
17 = 10 + 5 + 2	18 = (2 × 2) + (2 × 2) + 10
19 = (2 × 2) + 10 + 5	20 = (10 × 2)
21 = (10 × 2) + 1	22 = (10 × 2) + 2
23 = (10 × 2) + 2 + 1	24 = (10 × 2) + (2 × 2)
25 = (10 × 2) + 5	26 = (10 × 2) + 5 + 1
27 = (10 × 2) + 5 + 2	28 = (10 × 2) + (2 × 2) + (2 × 2)
29 = (10 × 2) + (2 × 2) + 5	30 = (10 × 2) + (5 × 2)

Technology Today
Habiba has spent £50 on mobile phone calls.
If Habiba spends £80 on mobile phone calls she will get 400 free texts.

Page 3

Money Matters

10p + 2p	(5p × 2) + 2p
10p + (1p × 2)	(5p × 2) + (1p × 2)
1p × 12	(1p × 10) + 2p
2p × 6	(1p × 8) + (2p × 2)
	(1p × 6) + (2p × 3)
5p + (1p × 7)	(1p × 4) + (2p × 4)
5p + 2p + (1p × 5)	(1p × 2) + (2p × 5)
5p + (2p × 2) + (1p × 3)	
5p + (2p × 3) + 1p	

Let's Investigate
Four different totals are possible: 27, 28, 29 and 30.

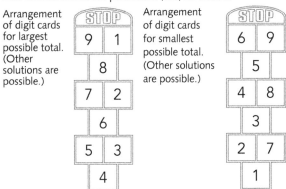

Arrangement of digit cards for largest possible total. (Other solutions are possible.)

Arrangement of digit cards for smallest possible total. (Other solutions are possible.)

Page 4

Technology Today
Total of all the digits in the left column is 12.
Total of all the digits in the middle column is 15.
Total of all the digits in the right column is 18.

Total of all the digits in the first row is 6.
Total of all the digits in the second row is 15.
Total of all the digits in the third row is 24.

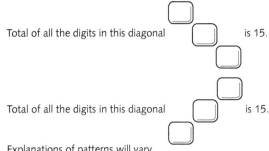

Total of all the digits in this diagonal is 15.

Total of all the digits in this diagonal is 15.

Explanations of patterns will vary.

The Puzzler

80 ÷ 8 = 10	9 × 5 = 45
42 ÷ 6 = 7	33 ÷ 3 = 11
400 ÷ 4 = 100	45 ÷ 9 = 5
7 × 10 = 70	100 ÷ 5 = 20

Inquisitive ant

inverse operation
A mathematical operation that reverses another operation. Addition is the inverse of subtraction, and vice versa; multiplication is the inverse of division, and vice versa.

Fractions

Prerequisites for learning

- Recognise, find, name and write fractions $\frac{1}{2}$, $\frac{1}{4}$ and $\frac{3}{4}$ of a length, shape, set of objects or quantity
- Write simple fractions, for example, $\frac{1}{2}$ of 6 = 3
- Choose and use appropriate standard units to estimate and measure length/height (m/cm); mass (kg/g) and capacity (litres/ml)
- Recognise and know the value of different denominations of coins and notes

Resources

pencil and paper
Resource sheet 2: My notes (optional)
Resource sheet 3: Pupil self assessment booklet (optional)
Resource sheet 9: Halves and quarters
Resource sheet 10: Fraction walls
Resource sheet 19: 1 cm squared paper
Resource sheet 20: 2 cm squared paper
ruler
several square pieces of paper
scissors
coloured pencils
modelling clay
weighing scales / balance
interlocking cubes
non-transparent bag or box

Teaching support

Page 1

Construct

- Children can undertake this activity either individually or in pairs.
- Tell the children to be as accurate as possible in their cutting of the shapes. Encourage them to fold and cut and / or use a ruler to draw lines and then cut.
- Some children may realise that they can divide the shapes into many small parts, for example, tenths, twelfths, sixteenths, … . If this is the case, do not expect them to divide the shapes into these fractions, rather, discuss these possibilities with them.

Let's Investigate

- Writing a list of objects that are ruined if they are cut in half is easier than writing a list of objects that are not ruined. Therefore, encourage the children to include more objects in the latter list.
- Items on the lists may include:
  - ruined: chair, tree, money, t-shirt …
  - just as good: fruit, vegetables, sandwich, paper, pencil …
- When individual children have written lists of a suitable length, arrange the children into pairs to compare and discuss their lists.

Page 2

Let's Investigate

- If necessary, draw children's attention to duplicated patterns, e.g.
- When individual children have drawn as many patterns as they think are possible, arrange the children into pairs to compare and discuss their patterns.

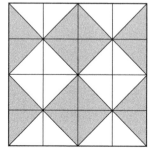
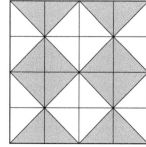

What's the Problem?

- To most accurately divide the lump of modelling clay in halves and quarters, children need to weigh the modelling clay. However, do not make this suggestion to them, nor provide them with the necessary equipment to do this. Let them discover this for themselves.

Page 3

Looking for Patterns

- Some children may need assistance with recording their tiles on squared paper.
- For the first part of this activity, ensure children realise that the tiles shown are the only possible ways of cutting the tiles into halves and quarters and that any other ways that they may think of are simply transformations of these four, for example:

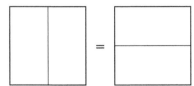 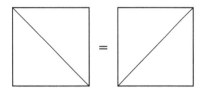

- For the second part of this activity, remind the children to look out for duplications of tile patterns, for example:

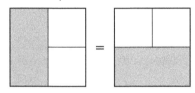 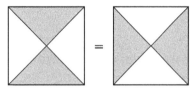

Looking for Patterns

- To help identify the rule for each sequence, suggest the children look at the difference between consecutive numbers in the sequence, e.g.

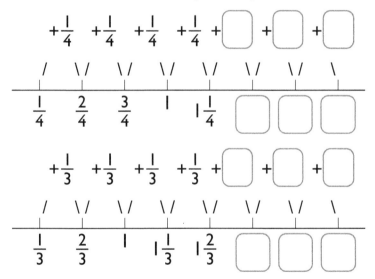

- An important aspect of this activity is for the children to look at the first and last number lines and to identify that $\frac{2}{4}$ and $\frac{1}{2}$ are the same (equivalent) fractions.

Page 4

Let's Investigate

- Before the children go off to work independently on this activity, ensure they understand that the top row of each fraction wall represents one whole, that the middle row has been divided into halves, and that the bottom row has been divided into quarters.

whole			
half ($\frac{1}{2}$)		half ($\frac{1}{2}$)	
quarter ($\frac{1}{4}$)	quarter ($\frac{1}{4}$)	quarter ($\frac{1}{4}$)	quarter ($\frac{1}{4}$)

- To complete the last three fraction walls successfully children need to know the equivalence between units of measurement. Therefore, you may need to remind the children that there are 1000 grams in 1 kg, 24 hours in 1 day and 12 in a dozen.
- Encourage the children to think of 'challenging amounts' for the last two fraction walls and not choose amounts that are relatively simple.
- When children have completed their sheets, arrange them into pairs or groups to share, compare and discuss their results.

Let's Investigate

- If appropriate, discuss the concept of equivalent fractions with the children, and how fractions can be reduced, i.e. $\frac{4}{12} = \frac{1}{3}$.
- Tell the children to add 12 green cubes to the bag or box. They then take out 8 / 10 / 12 cubes and say how many of each colour they have and what fraction of 8 / 10 / 12 cubes this is.

AfL

- What are some of the ways that you can divide a square into equal pieces?
- Explain to me how this square has been half coloured.
- How did you make sure that your piece of modelling clay was divided exactly in half? What did you do to make sure that it was divided equally into quarters?
- Use fractions to describe this tile pattern to me.
- How did you work out the next three numbers in this pattern? What would be the next number?
- How did you work out half / one-quarter of this amount?
- Look at this group of cubes. There are three different coloured cubes. What fraction of the cubes are ...? What fraction are ...? What fraction are ...? What fraction of these cubes are ... and ...?

Answers

Page 1

Construct
Shapes will vary.

Let's Investigate
Lists will vary.

Page 2

Let's Investigate
Patterns will vary.

What's the Problem?
Results of the investigation will vary.

Page 3

Looking for Patterns
Patterned tiles will vary.

Looking for Patterns

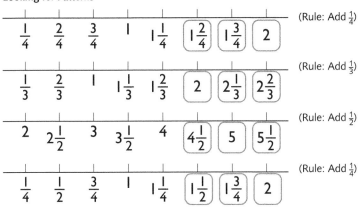

(Rule: Add $\frac{1}{4}$)
(Rule: Add $\frac{1}{3}$)
(Rule: Add $\frac{1}{2}$)
(Rule: Add $\frac{1}{4}$)

The first and last number lines both involve adding $\frac{1}{4}$. They also show that $\frac{2}{4}$ and $\frac{1}{2}$ are equivalent.

Page 4

Let's Investigate

20p	
10p	10p

5p	5p	5p	5p

£1	
50p	50p

25p	25p	25p	25p

32 litres	
16 l	16 l

8 l	8 l	8 l	8 l

1 kg	
500 g	500 g

250 g	250 g	250 g	250 g

1 day	
12 hr	12 hr

6 hr	6 hr	6 hr	6 hr

1 dozen eggs	
6 eggs	6 eggs

3 eggs	3 eggs	3 eggs	3 eggs

The last two fraction walls will vary.

Let's Investigate
Results of the investigation will vary.

Inquisitive ant

dozen
A group or set of 12.

Issue 19

Fractions

Prerequisites for learning

- Recognise, find, name and write fractions $\frac{1}{2}$, $\frac{1}{4}$ and $\frac{3}{4}$ of a length, shape, set of objects or quantity
- Write simple fractions, for example, $\frac{1}{2}$ of 6 = 3
- Understand that halving is the inverse of doubling and derive and recall doubles of all numbers to at least 20, and the corresponding halves
- Recall and use multiplication and division facts for the 2 and 4 multiplication tables
- Recognise multiples of 2 and 4
- Recognise the equivalence of $\frac{2}{4}$ and $\frac{1}{2}$

Resources

pencil and paper
Resource sheet 2: My notes (optional)
Resource sheet 3: Pupil self assessment booklet (optional)
Resource sheet 9: Halves and quarters
Resource sheet 11: Eighths
ruler
red, blue, green and yellow coloured pencils
several circular pieces of paper
scissors
selection of fruit such as tangerines, satsumas, clementines, oranges, …
plate

Teaching support

Page 1

The Language of Maths

- Remind the children that they are required to think of everyday examples of how and when we describe something using the language of fractions.

  Examples may include:

  – money: half price

  – time: half past, quarter past / to

  – other measures: half a litre / kilogram / mile

  – music: half / quarter / eighth notes

  – sport: half-time.

- When individual children have written a suitable number of examples, arrange the children into pairs to compare and discuss their lists.

Let's Investigate

- Remind the children that as they think of numbers to write on their lists they should think carefully about those numbers that belong to more than one list.

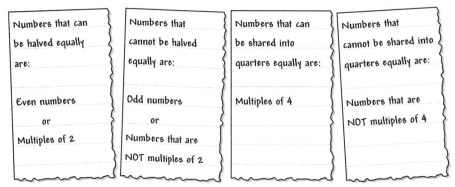

Numbers that can be halved equally are:	Numbers that cannot be halved equally are:	Numbers that can be shared into quarters equally are:	Numbers that cannot be shared into quarters equally are:
Even numbers or Multiples of 2	Odd numbers or Numbers that are NOT multiples of 2	Multiples of 4	Numbers that are NOT multiples of 4

- When individual children have written a suitable number of numbers in all four lists, arrange the children into pairs to compare and discuss their lists.
- Encourage the children to write three-digit numbers on their lists.
- Once the children have completed this activity, ask them to comment on the common properties between each group of numbers.

Page 2

The Puzzler

- It is envisaged the children will show their answers to these two puzzles on their copy of the issue.

- Encourage the children to be as accurate as possible in their drawing of the four straight lines.

Let's Investigate

- This practical activity introduces children to eighths and the equivalence between $\frac{2}{8}$ and $\frac{1}{4}$.

- The most important aspect of this activity is for the children to realise that in each large rectangle there are the same number of red and blue small rectangles shaded, and therefore two-eighths ($\frac{2}{8}$) must be the same as, or equivalent to, one-quarter ($\frac{1}{4}$).

- Before children go off to work independently on this activity you may wish to discuss an example with them, e.g.

 or

- If necessary, provide the children with an additional copy of Resource sheet 11: Eighths.

- Using another copy of Resource sheet 11: Eighths, ask the children to shade:

  – $\frac{1}{2}$ red

  – $\frac{1}{8}$ blue

  – $\frac{3}{8}$ green.

Page 3

Construct

- Children can undertake this activity either individually or in pairs.

- Tell the children to be as accurate as possible in their cutting of the circles. Encourage them to fold and cut and / or use a ruler to draw lines and then cut.

- Some children may realise that they can divide the circles into many small parts, for example, eighths, twelfths, sixteenths, … . If this is the case, do not expect them to divide the circles into these fractions, rather, discuss these possibilities with them.

Let's Investigate

- It is recommended that children work in pairs or small groups for this activity so that they can share ideas and discuss their reasoning.

- Children can write about their findings individually, in pairs or in groups. Remind the children that they are expected to write about what fraction of the whole fruit is one / two / three / four … segment(s).

Page 4

Let's Investigate

- If necessary, draw children's attention to duplicated patterns, e.g.

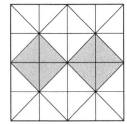 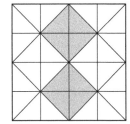

- When individual children have drawn as many patterns as they think are possible, arrange the children into pairs to compare and discuss their patterns.

At Home

- Ensure children understand that the fractions which are used to describe the amount of cloud cover in the sky can only be considered approximations.

- Once the children have completed the investigation, ensure that there is an opportunity in class for pairs or groups of children to discuss their results.

AfL

- Tell me some numbers you wrote on your list of numbers that can be halved equally. What were some of the numbers that can be shared into quarters equally?
- Tell me some numbers that were on more than one list. Why was this?
- On what list would you write the number 27? What about the number 16 / 40?
- What did you think about when you were deciding how to cut these cakes?
- What do you notice about the number of red squares and the number of blue squares you coloured on each of the rectangles? So what can you tell me about one-quarter and two-eighths?
- What are some of the ways that you can divide a circle into equal pieces?
- Use fractions to describe this many segments of the total satsuma.
- How does this pattern show one-quarter of the large square?

Answers

Page 1

The Language of Maths
Lists will vary.

Let's Investigate
Lists will vary.

Page 2

The Puzzler

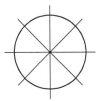 

Let's Investigate
Rectangles will vary.

Page 3

Construct
Shapes will vary.

Let's Investigate
Findings will vary.

Page 4

Let's Investigate
Patterns will vary.

At Home
Results of the investigation will vary.

Inquisitive ant
share equally
To divide a number or quantity into equal parts.

Fractions

Prerequisites for learning

- Recognise, find, name and write fractions $\frac{1}{2}$, $\frac{1}{4}$ and $\frac{3}{4}$ of a length, shape, set of objects or quantity
- Write simple fractions, for example, $\frac{1}{2}$ of 6 = 3
- Read and write unit and non-unit fractions, e.g. $\frac{1}{3}$, $\frac{9}{10}$, interpreting the denominator as the parts of a whole and the numerator as the number of parts
- Find unit fractions of numbers and quantities
- Use mental methods of calculation with fractions

Resources

pencil and paper
Resource sheet 2: My notes (optional)
Resource sheet 3: Pupil self assessment booklet (optional)
tape measure
calculator (optional)

Teaching support

Page 1

The Puzzler

- It is recommended that children have completed the Inquisitive ant task before starting on this activity.
- If appropriate, discuss the concept of equivalent fractions with the children, and how fractions can be reduced, i.e. $\frac{4}{10} = \frac{2}{5}$.
- Ask the children to use fractions to make other statements to describe the faces, for example, 'Three-tenths of the faces are wearing a hat.'

Page 2

Sports Update

- Encourage the children to draw a diagram.
- If half of the balls are tennis balls, then all of the other balls must be half of the total as $\frac{1}{2} + \frac{1}{2} = 1$.

ⓉⓉⓉⓉⓉⓉⓉⓉⓉⓉⓉⓉ
ⒻⒻⒻⒻⒻⒻⒻⓈⓈⓈⒷⒷ

What's the Problem?

- Encourage the children to be systematic in setting out their work, e.g.

Day	Starts with	Ends with
Monday	64	32
Tuesday	32	16
Wednesday	16	8
Thursday	8	4
Friday	4	2
Saturday	2	1

Page 3

Money Matters

- Tell the children to work out the fractions in the order in which they are presented.
- Children should find it relatively easy to work out a half and one-quarter of £120 (£60 / £30). They can then work out the remainder simply by subtracting the £90 (£60 + £30) from £120 (to leave £30). Then, knowing that as Sam and Lee each receive the same amount, all they need do is work out a half of £30 to know how much they each receive (£15).

The Arts Roundup

- One-third of the theatre holds 40 people, so the whole theatre holds three times this number:
  $3 \times 40 = 120$ people.
- On Wednesday it is only one-quarter full: $\frac{1}{4} \times 120 = 30$, so there are 30 people watching the show on Wednesday.

- Referring to the illustration in the issue, you may wish to suggest to the children that they count the number of rows of seats in the theatre, work out how many rows make $\frac{1}{4}$ of the theatre, and then multiply by 10 to get the number of seats.

Page 4

Let's Investigate

- Ensure that children understand that they are looking for something only approximately $\frac{1}{2}, \frac{1}{4}, \frac{1}{5}$ or $\frac{1}{3}$ their height.

Let's Investigate

- It is recommended that children have completed the Inquisitive ant task before starting on this activity.
- This activity introduces children, in a practical way, to the addition of fractions with like denominators. If appropriate, show the children how to write these addition calculations, for example, $\frac{7}{10} + \frac{3}{10} = \frac{10}{10} = 1$
- Tell the children that there are four pairs of fractions that make a whole and four sets of three fractions that make a whole.

AfL

- Using fractions, describe this group of faces to me. How else can you describe them?
- What did you do to work out the answer to this problem / solve this puzzle? What could you have done differently? Would it have been better? Why?
- What calculations did you need to do to get this answer?
- How did you know that the … is approximately a half / one-third / one-quarter / one-fifth your height?
- How do you know that these two / three fractions make a whole?

Answers

Page 1

The Puzzler

4 faces have a round face. This is $\frac{4}{10}$ ($\frac{2}{5}$) of the faces.

7 faces have their eyes open. This is $\frac{7}{10}$ of the faces.

6 faces are happy. This is $\frac{6}{10}$ ($\frac{3}{5}$) of the faces.

8 faces have hair. This is $\frac{8}{10}$ ($\frac{4}{5}$) of the faces.

1 face is sad and wearing a hat. This is $\frac{1}{10}$ of the faces.

3 faces have hair and are wearing glasses. This is $\frac{3}{10}$ of the faces.

Page 2

Sports Update

There are 12 tennis balls in the PE cupboard.
Altogether there are 24 balls in the PE cupboard.
Explanations as to how the answers were worked out will vary.

What's the Problem?

There was one chocolate drop left on Saturday.

Page 3

Money Matters

Mrs Thomas will spend £60 on Tom, £30 on Lisa and £15 each on Sam and Lee.

The Arts Roundup

30 people were watching the show on Wednesday.

Page 4

Let's Investigate

Results of the investigation will vary.

Let's Investigate

Pairs of fractions that make a whole:	Groups of three fractions that make a whole:
$\frac{1}{10} + \frac{9}{10}$	$\frac{1}{10} + \frac{2}{10} + \frac{7}{10}$
$\frac{2}{10} + \frac{8}{10}$	$\frac{1}{10} + \frac{3}{10} + \frac{6}{10}$
$\frac{3}{10} + \frac{7}{10}$	$\frac{1}{10} + \frac{4}{10} + \frac{5}{10}$
$\frac{4}{10} + \frac{6}{10}$	$\frac{2}{10} + \frac{3}{10} + \frac{5}{10}$

Inquisitive ant one tenth
One of ten equal parts of something.

Issue 21

Length and height

Prerequisites for learning

- Choose and use appropriate standard units to estimate and measure length/height in any direction (m/cm) to the nearest appropriate unit, using suitable measuring instruments
- Read the numbered divisions on a scale and interpret the divisions between them
- Use a ruler to draw and measure lines to the nearest centimetre
- Add, subtract, multiply and divide numbers using concrete objects, pictorial representations, and mentally
- Make estimations and approximations

Resources

pencil and paper

Resource sheet 2: My notes (optional)

Resource sheet 3: Pupil self assessment booklet (optional)

individual and group skipping rope

stick

tape measure

calculator (optional)

trundle wheel (optional)

interlocking cubes

Teaching support

Page 1

In the Past

- It is recommended that children work in pairs or small groups for this activity so that they can share ideas and discuss their reasoning.

Focus on Science

- Tell the children that there is one piece of information in the question that is not really needed in order to work out the answer. Can they identify this piece of information ('…but shorter than the beech')?

Page 2

Sports Update

- Ensure the children realise that they are only expected to find out approximately how many skipping ropes there are in the school and estimate the total length of all the skipping ropes.
- This activity assumes that there are just two different lengths of skipping rope in a school. If this is not the case, then you will need to discuss this with the children.

Focus on Science

- It is recommended that, if possible, children complete this activity and the In the Past activity on page 3 together as both activities explore different methods for measuring the height of a tree and other tall objects. However, unlike the activity on page 3, it needs to be a clear sunny day in order for the children to do this activity.
- Of the two activities, this is the more complex and difficult. Most children will require the use of a calculator to successfully work out the height of the tree and other tall objects.
- If the children complete both activities and use the two different methods for measuring the height of a tree and other tall objects, ensure that there is an opportunity for them to compare the two methods.

Page 3

In the Past

- It is recommended that children complete this activity and the Focus on Science activity on page 2 together as both activities explore different methods for measuring the height of a tree and other tall objects.
- Of the two activities, this is the easier.

- If the children complete both activities and use the two different methods for measuring the height of a tree and other tall objects, ensure that there is an opportunity for them to compare the two methods.
- If appropriate, allow the children to use a trundle wheel to measure the distance from the base of the tree.

The Language of Maths

- Once children have completed the activity, arrange them in pairs and compare and discuss their lists.
- If appropriate, discuss with the children the two different measuring systems for length: metric and imperial.

Page 4

Sports Update

- You may need to spend time discussing this activity with the children before they go off to work independently on finding out the answers to the questions.
- If necessary, allow the children to use a calculator.

Let's Investigate

- There are two aspects to this investigation. Firstly, estimating how many interlocking cubes are needed to build a wall 2 metres long and 1 cube high, and then building the wall to check the estimation. Secondly, estimating how tall a wall can be built using interlocking cubes before it falls down, and then building the wall to check the estimation.
- For the first part of the investigation, discuss with the children how they do not need to build a wall 2 metres long to work out how many cubes are needed. Explain that by building a wall a quarter or a half of a metre long, and counting how many cubes they have used to do this, they can then scale up this amount to work out the total number of interlocking cubes needed.

AfL

- How could I measure the length of the playground without using a measuring tape? Why wouldn't this method be a good one?
- How did you solve this problem / puzzle?
- How did you work out the total length of skipping rope in our school? How close to the actual answer do you think this is? Why?
- Which method for measuring the height of a tree do you think is the best? Why do you think that?
- What calculations did you need to do to work out the answer to this problem?
- How close was your estimate to the actual number?

Answers

Page 1

In the Past
Methods and explanations will vary.

Focus on Science
poplar: 12 metres
beech: 9 metres
elm: $7\frac{1}{2}$ metres
pine: 6 metres
yew: 6 metres

Page 2

Sports Update
Results of the investigation will vary.

Focus on Science
Results of the investigation will vary.

Page 3

In the Past
Results of the investigation will vary.

The Language of Maths
Lists will vary.

Page 4

Sports Update
Three laps of the track are 600 m.

Five laps of the track total 1 km.

Each runner runs half way round the track.
The total distance of the 4 × 100 relay race is 400 m, which is two laps of the track.

Each runner runs two laps of the track.
The total distance of the 4 × 400 relay race is 1600 m (1 km 600 m or 1.6 km), which is eight laps of the track.

Let's Investigate
Results of the investigation will vary.

Inquisitive ant

distance
The length of space between two people, places or things.

Mass

Prerequisites for learning

- Choose and use appropriate standard units to estimate and measure mass (kg/g) to the nearest appropriate unit, using suitable measuring instruments
- Read the numbered divisions on a scale
- Add, subtract, multiply and divide numbers using concrete objects, pictorial representations, and mentally
- Make estimations and approximations
- Solve logic puzzles

Resources

pencil and paper

Resource sheet 2: My notes (optional)

Resource sheet 3: Pupil self assessment booklet (optional)

kitchen scales

bathroom scales

balance and a 500 g ($\frac{1}{2}$ kg) weight

container of interlocking cubes

container of pennies

container of marbles

container of counters

0 – 9 dice

Teaching support

Page 1

What's the Problem?

- Children should have had experience of other logic problems before attempting this problem.

Focus on Science

- This activity is intended to be very open-ended and left up to the children's imagination and interpretation, especially in respect to the terms 'smaller' and 'larger'. It is recommended that children work in pairs or small groups for this activity so that they can share ideas and discuss their reasoning.
- What is most important about this activity is the explanations and reasoning that children offer.

Page 2

At Home

- Once the children have completed the investigation, ensure that there is an opportunity in class for pairs or groups of children to discuss and compare their lists.

At Home

- Once the children have completed the investigation, ensure that there is an opportunity in class for pairs or groups of children to discuss and compare their lists.

Page 3

The Puzzler

- Some children may need assistance when calculating with the $\frac{1}{4}$ kg and $\frac{1}{2}$ kg weights.
- Ask the children to choose different combinations of the weights displayed in the issue and draw their own balancing scales, for example:

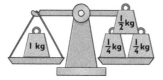

Let's Investigate

- The purpose of this activity is for the children to realise that, when they are holding an object, their mass will be the mass of themselves plus the mass of the object, but if the object is light, the bathroom scales will not detect the extra mass.

- Can the children work out the approximate minimum mass that an object needs to be before it will register on the bathroom scales? What does this mean about the accuracy of the mass of objects measured?

Page 4

The Language of Maths

- Once children have completed the activity, arrange them in pairs to compare and discuss their lists.
- If appropriate, discuss with the children the two different measuring systems for mass: metric and imperial.

Let's Investigate

- As the children play the game, discuss with them their predictions as to which game will take the shortest / longest time to play and why this is.

AfL

- How did you go about solving this problem / puzzle?
- How are you the same as / different from a baby elephant?
- Tell me what you found out at home / in the supermarket.
- Did the readings on the bathroom scales always increase when you were holding an object? Why not?
- Which game was the quickest / longest to play? Why was this?

Answers

Page 1

What's the Problem?
Apples weigh 3 kg.
Oranges weigh 1 ½ kg.
Bananas weigh 2 kg.
Pears weigh 1 kg.

Focus on Science
Answers will vary.

Page 2

At Home
Results of the investigation will vary.

At Home
Results of the investigation will vary.

Page 3

The Puzzler

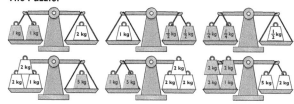

Let's Investigate
When children are holding an object, their mass will be the mass of themselves plus the mass of the object.

If the object is light, the bathroom scales will not detect the extra mass.

Page 4

The Language of Maths
Lists will vary.

Let's Investigate
Results will vary. However, the game that used the lightest objects should have been the slowest, and the game that used the heaviest objects should have been the quickest.

Inquisitive ant

mass
The amount of matter that an object contains.

Issue 23

Capacity and volume

Prerequisites for learning

- Choose and use appropriate standard units to estimate and measure volume/capacity (litres/ml) to the nearest appropriate unit, using suitable measuring instruments
- Read the numbered divisions on a scale
- Add, subtract, multiply and divide numbers using concrete objects, pictorial representations, and mentally
- Make estimations and approximations

Resources

pencil and paper

Resource sheet 2: My notes (optional)

Resource sheet 3: Pupil self assessment booklet (optional)

large, clear, plastic calibrated measuring jug half full of water, e.g. 1 or 2 litre jug

collection of waterproof objects that will fit into the measuring jug

selection of containers ranging from less than 0·5 litres to over 2 litres

cup

range of different containers larger than the cup, e.g. jugs, bottles, yoghurt pots

access to water

funnel

interlocking cubes

selection of different commercially available construction materials

coloured pencils

Teaching support

Page 1

Focus on Science

- This activity is designed to introduce two concepts to the children. Firstly, that objects either float or sink. Secondly and more importantly for the purpose of this activity, for the objects that sink, the notion of displacement and that the larger an object is, the greater the rise in water level.
- Ensure that the children choose objects that will both float and sink, preferably more of the latter. If necessary, you may wish to provide the objects to use to ensure that a range of different objects are chosen.
- It is recommended that the children complete this activity before working on the Focus on Science activity on page 4. You may also want the children to do these two activities one immediately after the other.

The Language of Maths

- Once children have completed the activity, arrange them in pairs to compare and discuss their definitions.
- If appropriate, discuss with the children the two different measuring systems for capacity: metric and imperial.

Page 2

Let's Investigate

- If appropriate, ask the children to repeat this activity at home.

- If the children do repeat this activity at home, ensure that there is an opportunity in class for pairs or groups of children to discuss their results and compare them with the results they got when they undertook the activity in school.

At Home

- Children investigate how much water is wasted if they leave the tap running while washing their hands.
- Once the children have completed the investigation, ensure that there is an opportunity in class for pairs or groups of children to discuss their results.

Page 3

Let's Investigate

- This activity may not be practical in all schools. However, if it is at all possible, enlist the help of the school caretaker to undertake this activity. It will provide the children with practical experience of water usage.

Let's Investigate

- This activity is designed to develop children's estimation skills when dealing with volume.

Page 4

Construct

- Once individuals or pairs of children have made their boxes, arrange the children into groups and ask each child / pair to offer their 'best' box, giving an explanation as to why they consider it to be the best.

Focus on Science

- It is recommended that the children have completed the 🔬 Focus on Science activity on page 1 before starting on this activity. You may also want the children to do these two activities one immediately after the other.

AfL

- What happens to the water level in a jug when you place something else in the jug with the water? How is this change in water level different for different objects?
- Tell me some containers in the classroom that hold between half a litre and one litre. What about some containers that hold more than two litres? According to your table, which type of containers do we have the most / least of? Why do you think this is?
- How did you work out how much water you waste if you leave the tap running while brushing your teeth? Why is this only an approximation?
- What did you and … (the school caretaker) find out?
- Which design of box is best? Why do you think it is this one?
- Tell me the results of your experiment. How accurate do you think your results are?

Answers

Page 1

Focus on Science
Results of the investigation will vary. However, children should realise that the objects either float or sink and for those objects that sink, the resulting rise in the water level depends upon the size of the object – the larger the object, the greater the rise in the water level.

The Language of Maths
Volume is a measure of how big something is in three dimensions.
Capacity describes how much space is inside a container. The capacity of a container is the maximum amount of liquid that it can hold.
Definitions will vary.

Page 2

Let's Investigate
Results of the investigation will vary.

At Home
Results of the investigation will vary.

Page 3

Let's Investigate
Results of the investigation will vary.

Let's Investigate
Results of the investigation will vary.

Page 4

Construct
Designs and explanations will vary.

Focus on Science
Results of the investigation will vary.

Inquisitive ant

displacement
The amount of liquid that is forced to move as the result of floating or submerging an object in the liquid.

Issue 24

Time

Prerequisites for learning

- Use units of time (minutes, hours, days, weeks, months) and know the relationships between them
- Tell and write the time to five minutes, including quarter past/to the hour and draw the hands on a clock face to show these times
- Compare and sequence intervals of time
- Make estimations and approximations
- Use a calendar
- Solve logic puzzles

Resources

pencil and paper

Resource sheet 2: My notes (optional)

Resource sheet 3: Pupil self assessment booklet (optional)

newspaper or magazine showing television listings

stopwatch

material for constructing a 1 minute sand timer, i.e. plastic bottle, sand, sticky tape

calendar

large sheet of paper

markers

ruler

scissors

computer (optional)

Teaching support

Page 1

What's the Problem?

- Suggest the children start with the clue about Patricia and end with the clue about Stanley.

Let's Investigate

- There are two aspects to this activity. Firstly, designing a television schedule for both children and secondly, writing an explanation as to which child watches more television each week.

- In order to successfully complete this activity, children need to be able to read 12-hour digital time and identify time intervals, including those that cross the hour. If necessary, look at the television schedule with the children and work through several examples. Ensure the children are able to calculate the length of a television programme.

- Some children may need assistance in organising their work. If appropriate, suggest they draw a table, for example:

Programme	Start time	Finish time	Length of programme

- If appropriate, allow the children to write their schedules using ICT.

Page 2

The Arts Roundup

- Ensure that the children are systematic with their completion of the calendar, realising that the dates mentioned are inclusive. Also tell the children to take particular care when an event crosses into the next month.

- Once the children have completed their calendar, arrange them in pairs and ask them to compare and check their calendars. When they have done this and come to an agreement, allow them to work together to find out how many days in the year there is / is not a performance in the theatre.

Page 3

The Language of Maths

- Once children have completed the activity, arrange them in pairs to compare and discuss their lists.
- If appropriate, discuss with the children the similarities and differences between analogue and 12-hour digital time. If children make reference to it, you may also want to discuss with them 24-hour notation.

What's the Problem

- Assist the children in using the calendar to work out the solution to the puzzle, e.g.

  ✕ water flowers

  ◯ weed garden

  ▨ cut grass

Page 4

Construct

- Be aware that this activity may take the children some time to complete and will require the use of a range of different resources. However, it is extremely worthwhile affording the time for this as it involves children using the skills of estimation and approximation, trial and improvement and perseverance in order to achieve a suitable degree of accuracy.
- Encourage the children to be as accurate as possible in making their sand timer exactly 1 minute long.

Construct

- You may wish to discuss this activity with the children before they go off to work independently. How are the children going to design their calendar? How much space will they leave to write entries on their calendar? Are they going to include the weekends on their calendar?
- The children will probably need to have access to a current calendar to record the dates for the half term.
- Suggest the children design their classroom calendar using ICT.
- A possible class calendar may look similar to the following:

June

Monday	Tuesday	Wednesday	Thursday	Friday
6 First day of term	7	8	9	10
13	14	15	16	17
20	21	22	23	24
27	28	29	30	

July

Monday	Tuesday	Wednesday	Thursday	Friday
				1
4	5	6	7	8
11	12	13	14	15
18	19	20	21	22 Last day of term

AfL

- How did you work out the answer to this problem?
- Talk me through your schedule. So who watches more television each week?
- According to this calendar what day of the week is the 16th September? Can you tell me another date in September that is also a Wednesday?
- What has this word to do with time?
- Tell me about some of the things on your list.
- How did you work out the day that Steve had to do all three jobs in the garden?
- Talk me through how you made your one-minute timer. Why did you choose to use … to make your timer? What else could you have used?
- What things did you have to think about when designing your class calendar?

Answers

Page 1

What's the Problem?
Leo is 8 years old, Stanley is 16, Patricia is 12 and Janet is 6.

Let's Investigate
Answers will vary depending on the length of the TV programmes that children choose.

Page 2

The Arts Roundup
245 days of the year there is a performance in the Meroo Opera Theatre.
120 days of the year there is no performance in the Theatre.

Page 3

The Language of Maths
Lists will vary.

What's the Problem?
The next time Steve will have to water the flowers, weed the garden and cut the grass is on 2nd June.

Page 4

Construct
Sand timers will vary.

Construct
Class calendars will vary.

Inquisitive ant calendar
A chart showing the days, weeks and months of a particular year.

Issue 25

Measurement

Prerequisites for learning

- Choose and use appropriate standard units to estimate and measure length/height in any direction (m/cm); mass (kg/g); temperature (°C); volume/capacity (litres/ml) to the nearest appropriate unit, using suitable measuring instruments
- Read the numbered divisions on a scale and interpret the divisions between them
- Compare and sequence intervals of time

Resources

pencil and paper

Resource sheet 2: My notes (optional)

Resource sheet 3: Pupil self assessment booklet (optional)

ball

tape measure

several sheets of paper of differing sizes

6 hard-boiled eggs (optional)

daily newspaper for one week

Teaching support

Page 1

Let's Investigate

- Prior to the children beginning the experiment, you may need to discuss with them how they are going to judge which is the furthest distance. Does it mean that when the ball is thrown at this distance the catcher never drops it? Or does it mean that when the ball is thrown at this distance that for the majority of the time the catcher catches it?

- Ensure the children write about their experiment and their results. One of the most important aspects of this activity is the justification that children give to the conclusions they make.

What's the Problem?

- It is the first part of this activity that some children may have difficulty with. If necessary, suggest the children draw and label a diagram, e.g.

Page 2

Focus on Science

- If necessary, remind children of the different measures, e.g. length, weight, capacity, time, temperature, area, perimeter, money.

- Once children have completed the activity, arrange them in pairs to compare and discuss their lists.

The Language of Maths

- Children write three or four exaggerated measures statements of their own. They then swap with a friend and rewrite the statements making them more realistic. When each child has done this, they then compare and discuss each exaggerated and realistic statement.

Page 3

Around the World

- While children will probably be able to easily find out who in their class travels the furthest and shortest distances to get to school, they may have some difficulty in calculating how far these distances are. Discuss with the children how they only need to give an approximation of the various distances.

- You may wish to suggest to the children that they ask the other children in the class to find out from their parents how far they travel to school.

At Home

- Once the children have completed the investigation, ensure that there is an opportunity in class for pairs or groups of children to discuss their results.
- If it is considered more appropriate, the children can carry out this investigation in school. If this is the case it is recommended that the children use hard-boiled eggs for the experiment.

Page 4

Focus on Science

- It has generally been considered that it is impossible to fold a sheet of paper in half more than seven or eight times, irrespective of the size of the paper. The children will more than likely still find this to be the case. However, in 2002 Britney Gallivan from the USA proved that a sheet of paper could be folded as many as 12 times.

Focus on Science

- For this activity you will need to supply the children with a daily newspaper for the duration of one week.
- As this activity will take a week to complete, it is recommended that it is started on a Monday.
- On the first day of this activity, you may need to help the children locate the weather section in the newspaper and interpret the temperature readings as presented in the paper.
- Ensure children understand the concept of temperature and the terms 'minimum' and 'maximum'.

AfL

- Describe your experiment to me. What results did you find out? How do these results compare with other results? Why do you think they are different?
- How did you work out the answer to this problem / solution to this puzzle?
- Tell me some of the things that are on your list. Why did you include that?
- Why is this statement of Derek's wrong? What is a more realistic statement that Derek could have made?
- Tell me the results of your investigation. What did you do to find out all this?
- Describe to me how the temperature changed throughout the week.

Answers

Page 1

Let's Investigate
Results of the investigation will vary.

What's the Problem?
It takes Ted 14 minutes to cut all 8 lengths.
Each length is $\frac{1}{2}$m (50 cm) long.

Page 2

Focus on Science
Lists will vary.

The Language of Maths
Statements will vary.

Page 3

Around the World
Answers will vary.

At Home
Results of the investigation will vary.

Page 4

Focus on Science
Results of the investigation will vary.

Focus on Science
Results of the investigation will vary.

Inquisitive ant  degree
1. A unit of measurement for temperature.
2. A unit of measurement for angles.

Issue 26

Measurement

Prerequisites for learning

- Choose and use appropriate standard units to estimate and measure length/height in any direction (m/cm); mass (kg/g); temperature (°C); volume/capacity (litres/ml) to the nearest appropriate unit, using suitable measuring instruments
- Read the numbered divisions on a scale and interpret the divisions between them
- Add, subtract, multiply and divide numbers using concrete objects, pictorial representations, and mentally
- Compare and sequence intervals of time
- Know the number of hours in a day

Resources

pencil and paper

Resource sheet 2: My notes (optional)

Resource sheet 3: Pupil self assessment booklet (optional)

Resource sheet 19: 1 cm squared paper

Resource sheet 20: 2 cm squared paper

ruler

thermometer

selection of newspapers and magazines

large sheet of paper

scissors

glue

analogue clock (optional)

computer (optional)

data handling software (optional)

Teaching support

Page 1

The Puzzler

- The first, third and fourth bags are the same in each calculation, the only bag that changes is the second. The lightest bag weighs 2 kg, so it is possible to work out how much the other two bags weigh.
- Tell the children that the weight of each bag is less than 10 kg.

Sports Update

- Suggest the children draw a table, e.g.

Week	1	2	3	4	5	6	7	8	9	10	11
Distance (km)	2	3	4	5	6	7	8	9	10	11	12

Page 2

Around the World

- If necessary, remind children of the different measures, e.g. length, weight, capacity, time, temperature, area, perimeter, money.
- Once children have completed the activity, arrange them in pairs to compare and discuss their lists.

Focus on Science

- Children will need to have completed this activity before starting on the two activities on page 3.
- Ensure children understand the concept of temperature and how it is measured in degrees Fahrenheit (°F) or degrees Celsius (°C) using an instrument called a thermometer.
- In this activity all the thermometer readings are in degrees Celsius.
- Ask the children to write statements comparing the temperatures in two cities. For example, 'New York is 7 degrees warmer than London.' 'Paris is 8 degrees cooler than Rome.'

Page 3

The Language of Maths

- Children will need to have completed the 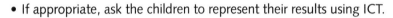 Focus on Science activity on page 2 before starting on this activity.
- This activity is designed to introduce children to the concept of negative numbers in the context of temperature.
- Allow the children to work in pairs to share their ideas of what the two temperature readings mean.

Focus on Science

- Children will need to have completed the Focus on Science activity on page 2 before starting on this activity.
- As this activity will take a week to complete, it is recommended that it is started on a Monday.
- Before the children carry out the investigation, ensure that they are able to read and interpret a thermometer.
- If appropriate, ask the children to represent their results using ICT.

Page 4

The Language of Maths

- Before the children go off to work independently on this activity you may need to look through a newspaper or magazine with them and provide them with several examples.
- If appropriate, do not expect the children to write what is being measured by each word. Simply finding 'measuring' words is sufficient.

What's the Problem?

- If necessary, discuss with the children that in 24 hours' time it will be midnight again. In (24 + 24) hours = 48 hours, it will be midnight again. In (48 + 24) hours = 72 hours it will be midnight again.
- Suggest the children use an analogue clock to help them calculate the time interval.

AfL

- How did you work out the value of that bag?
- Explain to me how you worked out the answer to this problem / solution to this puzzle.
- Tell me some of the things on your list. How did you sort your list? Could you sort the things on your list a different way?
- How do you read a thermometer? Which of these cities is the hottest / coldest? Which city is warmer / cooler than …?
- Tell me about how the temperature changed over the day in our classroom.
- Why did you choose to record your results in this way?

Answers

Page 1

The Puzzler

Sports Update
Tamsin has been running for between 10 and 11 weeks.

Page 2

Around the World
Lists and criteria for groups will vary.

Focus on Science
London 4 °C, New York 11 °C, Paris 17 °C, Rome 25 °C,
Edinburgh –2 °C, Moscow –8 °C

Page 3

The Language of Maths
Answers will vary.

Focus on Science
Results of the investigation will vary.

Page 4

The Language of Maths
Results of the investigation will vary.

What's the Problem?
No. It will be midnight again.

Inquisitive ant

scale
1. An instrument or device with graduated markings for measuring something.
2. A system of measurement based on a series of marks presented at regular intervals and representing numerical values.

2-D shapes

Prerequisites for learning

- Identify patterns and relationships involving shapes
- Visualise common 2-D shapes
- Identify shapes from pictures of them in different positions and orientations
- Sort, draw and describe shapes, referring to their properties

Resources

pencil and paper
Resource sheet 2: My notes (optional)
Resource sheet 3: Pupil self assessment booklet (optional)
Resource sheet 7: Squares
Resource sheet 12: Square jigsaws
Resource sheet 13: Making shapes
Resource sheet 21: Squared dot paper
ruler
scissors
matchsticks
geoboards and elastic bands

Teaching support

Page 1

The Puzzler

- If necessary, show the children how to draw the squares on squared dot paper.
- Ensure children realise that the solution to the last puzzle involves squares of different sizes (1 large square and 2 small squares).

Looking for Patterns

- There are four small squares, one medium square and one large square, making a total of six squares altogether.

Page 2

Let's Investigate

- This activity introduces children to tetrominoes (geometric shapes made from four congruent squares) and pentominoes (geometric shapes made from five congruent squares).
- Ensure children realise that, when forming their shapes, sides of adjoining squares must align, for example:

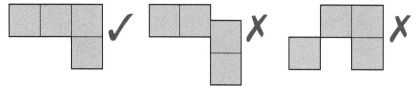

- Referring to the example in the issue, also ensure that the children are able to identify pairs of shapes that are transformations of each other. For example:

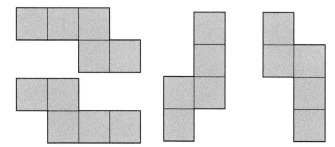

Looking for Patterns
- Tell the children that there are different combinations of triangles, squares and pentagons with a total of 9 / 10 / 11 / 12 and 13 sides. Can they find all the different combinations?

Page 3

Let's Investigate

- Ensure children accurately draw 3 × 3 and 4 × 4 squares on squared dot paper to show their solutions, i.e.

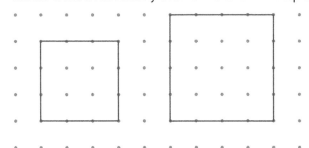

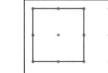
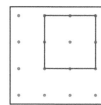

- Also ensure that children realise that these two squares are considered the same.

- Once children have completed the activity, arrange them in pairs to compare and discuss their solutions.

- Tell the children that there are five different sized squares possible on a 3 × 3 square, and eight different sized squares possible on a 4 × 4 square.

Construct

- You may wish to suggest to the children that they use a ruler to draw in all the sides of each of the shapes.

Page 4

Construct

- There are two parts to this activity. The first involves the children cutting up the two squares on Resource sheet 12: Square jigsaws, and then rearranging the pieces back into the two squares. The second part requires the children to create their own square shape jigsaw puzzles.
- Ensure that the children understand the rules for creating their own square shape jigsaw puzzle.

Let's Investigate

- There are two aspects to this activity. Firstly, arranging the shapes to see whether or not it is possible to make 3, 4, 5, 6, 7 and 8 sided shapes. Secondly, how to record the shapes created.
- Can the children arrange the shapes to make different types of quadrilaterals, e.g. square, rectangle, trapezium and parallelogram?

AfL

- Which was the easiest / hardest of these matchsticks puzzles? Why?
- Are all the squares in this puzzle the same size? How many different sized squares are there?
- How many different shapes did you make using 4 / 5 / 6 squares?
- Why are these two shapes the same?
- Is there another combination of shapes that has a total of 9 / 10 / 11 / 12 / 13 sides?
- How many different sized squares did you make? Is this all the different sized squares there are? How can you be sure?
- Why was it so easy to name each of these shapes?
- Was your friend able to complete your jigsaw? Did they find it easy or hard? How could you change your jigsaw to make it harder / easier?
- Was it possible to arrange these pieces to make a shape with 3 / 4 / 5 / 6 / 7 / 8 sides? How did you do it?

Answers

Page 1

The Puzzler

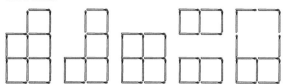

Other solutions are possible.

Looking for Patterns
There are six squares altogether.

Page 2

Let's Investigate
These are the five different four-square shapes.

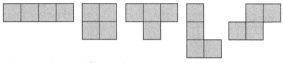

These are the 12 different five-square shapes.

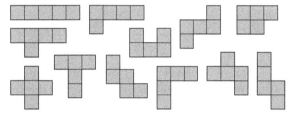

Looking for Patterns
Shapes with a total of 9 sides:
   3 triangles
   1 pentagon and 1 square.
Shapes with a total of 10 sides:
   2 pentagons
   2 triangles and 1 square.
Shapes with a total of 11 sides:
   2 squares and 1 triangle.
   1 pentagon and 2 triangles.
Shapes with a total of 12 sides:
   4 triangles
   3 squares
   1 pentagon, 1 square and 1 triangle.
Shapes with a total of 13 sides:
   1 pentagon and 2 squares
   2 pentagons and 1 triangle.

Page 3

Let's Investigate

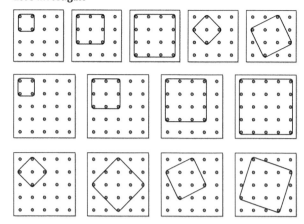

Construct
rectangle, triangle, star, pentagon and square.

Page 4

Construct

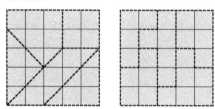

Children's jigsaws will vary.

Let's Investigate
Shapes will vary.

Inquisitive ant

vertex

The angular point of a polygon or polyhedron. Also referred to as a *corner*.

Issue 28

3-D shapes

Prerequisites for learning

- Identify patterns and relationships involving shapes
- Visualise common 3-D shapes
- Identify shapes from pictures of them in different positions and orientations
- Sort, make and describe shapes, referring to their properties

Resources

pencil and paper

Resource sheet 2: My Notes (optional)

Resource sheet 3: Pupil self assessment booklet (optional)

football

piece of chalk or some small stickers (optional)

junk such as cardboard boxes and other modelling material (optional)

interlocking cubes

Lego pieces (optional)

Teaching support

Page 1

Sports Update

- A football is not a sphere. It is actually a truncated icosahedron. It is made from 32 polygons: 12 regular pentagons and 20 regular hexagons.
- Some children may need assistance in being systematic when counting the number of 2-D shapes used to make a football to ensure that they do not over-count or under-count. If appropriate, provide them with a piece of chalk or some small stickers to mark / place on each shape once they have counted it.

Construct

- You may wish to suggest to the children that they use a ruler to draw in all the sides of each of the 3-D shapes.

Page 2

Sports Update

- Once the children have completed the activity, ask them to group the equipment they have located according to its shape. Which 3-D shape is used most in sports equipment?

Construct

- The purpose of this activity is for the children to design their robot, thinking of the different shapes needed for the different parts of the robot, and selecting the items of junk that are the appropriate shapes.
- If the resources are readily available, and time allows, the children could build their robot.

Page 3

Construct

- Ensure that the children realise there are two parts to this activity. Firstly, working out how many cubes were used to build each of the three models, and secondly, making and displaying a model for a friend.
- If necessary, for the first part of the activity, suggest the children construct each model using interlocking cubes. Ensure, however, that the children reproduce an exact replica of the models, including using those cubes that are needed to make the model but cannot be seen.
- Do the children notice that the second and third models are identical?
- Children can make their model using exactly 27 interlocking cubes, fewer than 27 cubes or more than 27 cubes.

The Language of Maths

- Using interlocking cubes all the same colour will make this activity easier. Using interlocking cubes of different colours will make this activity harder.

- You may need to work with the children in using the most appropriate and efficient wording for their set of instructions.

- Children construct a model using Lego pieces and write a set of instructions for making their model. They then give their partner a set of Lego pieces identical to those in their model, and ask their partner to make the model following the written instructions.

Page 4

The Language of Maths

- Prior to the activity, discuss with the children words and properties that might be appropriate to use when writing their descriptions, for example, face, corners (or vertices), edge, point, flat, curved, straight, round, … .

At Home

- Once the children have completed the investigation, ensure that there is an opportunity in class for pairs or groups of children to discuss their results.

AfL

- What shapes are used to make a football? How did you make sure that you counted all the shapes? How do you know that you haven't counted some of the shapes more than once?
- How did you know that this shape was a cube / cylinder …?
- What are all the different 3-D shapes that you found in the playground? Were there some shapes that you didn't know the name of? Can you describe this shape to me? What shape is it like? What shape do you think it might be? How could you find out the name of this shape?
- What are all the different shapes you used to construct your model robot? What shapes were really useful? Which shapes did you want to use but were hard to find examples of?
- Why do you think this model is made up of … cubes?
- Let me see if I can follow your instructions to make a model. What could you do to improve your instructions?
- Is this description precise enough to know that the solid is a cuboid and not a cube?
- Why do you think most batteries are cylindrical in shape?

Answers

Page 1

Sports Update
A football is not a perfect sphere. It is actually a truncated icosahedron. It is made from 32 polygons: 12 regular pentagons and 20 regular hexagons.

Construct
Cube, cylinder, pyramid and cone.

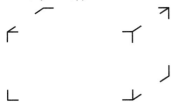

Page 2

Sports Update
Results of the investigation will vary.

Construct
Drawings will vary.

Page 3

Construct
All three models have 27 cubes.
Models will vary.

The Language of Maths
Instructions will vary.

Page 4

The Language of Maths
Descriptions will vary.

At Home
Results of the investigation will vary.

Inquisitive ant

3-D
Abbreviation of *three-dimensional*. A solid shape with dimensions of height, width and depth.

Prerequisites for learning

- Identify reflective symmetry in patterns and 2-D shapes
- Draw lines of symmetry in shapes
- Draw and complete shapes with reflective symmetry
- Draw the reflection of a shape in a mirror line along one side

Resources

pencil and paper

Resource sheet 2: My notes (optional)

Resource sheet 3: Pupil self assessment booklet (optional)

Resource sheet 14: Reflective square patterns

Resource sheet 15: Reflective circle patterns

four different coloured pencils

mirror

counters of the same colour (optional)

Teaching support

Page 1

Let's Investigate

- Ensure children understand the three different sizes of triangles, i.e.
- Children need one copy of Resource sheet 14: Reflective square patterns for this activity and an additional copy for the Let's Investigate activity on page 2.

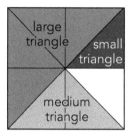

- In the first part of the activity, as the children are required to colour half of the large 4 × 4 squares, ensure that they realise they need to colour a total of eight small squares – four on one side of the line of symmetry and four on the other side of the line of symmetry.

- In the second part of the activity, ensure that the children realise they need to colour a total of eight medium triangles (or 16 small triangles) – four medium (or eight small) triangles on one side of the line of symmetry and four medium (or eight small) triangles on the other side of the line of symmetry.

- You may wish the children to work in pairs on this activity so that they can discuss the symmetrical properties of their designs.

- If appropriate, discuss with the children how some patterns can have both vertical and horizontal lines of symmetry, such as both examples in the issue.

- Ask the children to write about how one or more of their patterns shows reflective symmetry.

Page 2

The Language of Maths

- If the children have successfully reflected their name into the three boxes, when they turn their sheet of paper upside down their name should appear in the same orientation as in the top left-hand box, for example:

GABRIEL	ӀƎӀЯ𐌁 AƆ
ƆAB𐑯ӀEL	GABRIEL

- Ask the children to predict, then find out, what would happen if they wrote their names in a different order.

Let's Investigate

- Children need one copy of Resource sheet 14: Reflective square patterns, for this activity and an additional copy for the Let's Investigate activity on page 1.

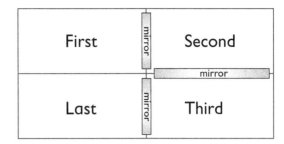

- You may wish the children to work in pairs on this activity so that they can discuss the symmetrical properties of their designs.

- Ask the children to write about how one or more of their patterns show reflective symmetry.

Page 3

The Language of Maths

- Children need to have completed this activity before starting on The Puzzler activity that follows.

- Encourage the children to record which letters show reflective symmetry using a similar method to that shown in the issue, i.e.

- Ask the children to sort the letters into four groups: those with no lines of symmetry, those with vertical symmetry, those with horizontal symmetry and those with vertical and horizontal symmetry.

- When the children have completed the activity, arrange them into pairs or groups to compare and discuss their results. Encourage the children to come up with a definitive list of those upper and lower case letters that show vertical and / or horizontal symmetry.

The Puzzler

- Children need to have successfully completed the previous activity, The Language of Maths, before starting this activity.

- Possible words that can be written horizontally include:
  BOX, CHOICE, DOCK, HIDE, HIKE, …

- Possible words that can be written vertically include:
  HAT, HIT, MOTH, TUMMY, WAIT, …

Page 4

Let's Investigate

- Children need one copy of Resource sheet 15: Reflective circle patterns, for this activity and an additional copy for the following Let's Investigate activity.

- You may wish the children to work in pairs on this activity so that they can discuss the symmetrical properties of their designs.

- If necessary, provide the children with a pile of small counters, all the same colour, so that they can try out potential patterns before drawing them on the Resource sheet.

- Ask the children to write about how one or more of their patterns shows reflective symmetry.

Let's Investigate

- Children need one copy of Resource sheet 15: Reflective circle patterns for this activity and an additional copy for the previous Let's Investigate activity.

- You may wish the children to work in pairs on this activity so that they can discuss the symmetrical properties of their designs.

- Ask the children to write about how one or more of their patterns shows reflective symmetry.

AfL

- How is your pattern symmetrical?
- Does your pattern have a vertical line of symmetry or a horizontal line of symmetry? How can you tell?
- Which letters of the alphabet are symmetrical? How is the letter A, C, M, … symmetrical?
- Can you colour two more squares / circles so that the pattern remains symmetrical? Can you colour three more squares / circles so that the pattern remains symmetrical? Why isn't it symmetrical now?

Answers

Page 1

Let's Investigate
Symmetrical patterns will vary.

Page 2

The Language of Maths
Results of the investigation will vary.

Let's Investigate
Symmetrical patterns will vary.

Page 3

The Language of Maths
Upper case letters with horizontal symmetry include:
B C D E H I K O X

Upper case letters with vertical symmetry include:
A H I M O T U V W X Y
Lower case letters with horizontal symmetry include:
a c l o x

Lower case letters with vertical symmetry include:
i l o t u v w x

The Puzzler

~~CHECK~~

~~BIKE~~

T O O T H

T O M M Y

Page 4

Let's Investigate
Symmetrical patterns will vary.

Let's Investigate
Symmetrical patterns will vary.

Inquisitive ant

line of symmetry
A straight line passing through the centre of a symmetrical shape or pattern.

Position and direction

Prerequisites for learning

- Follow and give instructions involving position, direction and movement
- Describe and identify the position of a square on a grid of squares
- Use the four compass directions
- Solve logic puzzles

Resources

pencil and paper

Resource sheet 2: My notes (optional)

Resource sheet 3: Pupil self assessment booklet (optional)

Resource sheet 16: Strange grids

Resource sheet 20: 2 cm squared paper

ruler

red, green, blue, yellow, black and purple coloured pencil

red, green, blue, yellow, black and purple counters (optional)

large world map

Teaching support

Page 1

The Puzzler

- Children should have had experience of other logic puzzles before attempting this puzzle.

- Provide the children with red, green, blue, yellow, black and purple counters and suggest they arrange and rearrange them on the stars until they find the solution. Then they colour the stars.

Page 2

The Language of Maths

- Using squared paper, children draw a route from a starting point to a finishing point using the same rules as in the issue:

  Rules:

  – You can only move left or right and up or down.

  – Diagonals are not allowed.

  – You can only move through a square on the grid once.

  – Lines on the route cannot cross.

  On a separate sheet of paper they then write the directions including the size of the grid (e.g. 5 × 5) and the location of 'Start' (e.g. top left square) and 'Finish' (e.g. bottom right square).

  Children then give their instructions for a friend to follow and use to draw the route.

  When complete, the children compare routes.

Page 3

The Language of Maths

- Ensure children are able to describe and identify the position of a square on a grid of squares.

The Language of Maths

- Ensure the children realise that, when writing their message in code, just like when writing a sentence, they must leave sufficient space between each word.

- Encourage the children to write a message of a similar length to the one written in the previous The Language of Maths activity.

• Also encourage the children to check that their secret message is correct and 'readable' before giving it to a friend to solve.

Page 4

Construct

• Children can use the grids on Resource sheet 16: Strange grids, to create their own picture / pattern. Perhaps drawing their picture / pattern on one of the grids and giving it to a friend to recreate on the other three grids.

Around the World

• Ensure the children understand and can use the four cardinal points of the compass.

• Ensure the children appreciate that they only need to find the approximate location of where they live. Some children may need assistance with this.

• Try and provide the children with a large map of the world for this activity. This way they will find it easier to locate countries or cities that are north, south, east and west of where they live.

• Introduce the children to the four intermediate or ordinal directions, i.e. north-east (NE), north-west (NW), south-west (SW), and south-east (SE), and ask them to find countries or cities that are in those directions from where they live.

AfL

• How do you know that this star should be red / blue … ?

• Describe this route to me.

• What are the coordinates for spelling your first name?

• Show me your strange grids. Which one do you like best? Why is that? What other strange grid could you have?

• Tell me a country / city that is north / south / east / west of where you live. Can you tell me another one? South-east means the direction between south and east. Can you tell me something that is south-east of where you live?

Answers

Page 1

The Puzzler

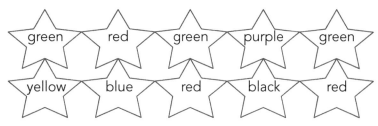

Page 2

The Language of Maths
Right 3
Down 2
Left 3
Down 1
Right 2
Down 1
Right 2

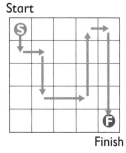

Page 3

The Language of Maths
The secret message reads: 'All spies to meet at classroom door at 1200 hours.'

The Language of Maths
Secret messages will vary.

Page 4

Construct

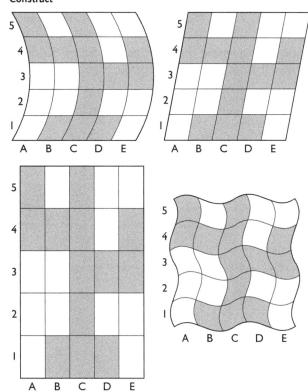

Around the World
Answers will vary.

Inquisitive ant

coordinates
A set of numbers (or letters and numbers) that together describe the exact position of something on a map or grid containing labelled axes.

Movement and angle

Prerequisites for learning

- Recognise and use whole, half and quarter turns, both clockwise and anticlockwise
- Know that a right angle represents a quarter turn

Resources

pencil and paper
Resource sheet 2: My notes (optional)
Resource sheet 3: Pupil self assessment booklet (optional)
scrap of paper
several sheets of A4 paper
coloured pencils
counters in two different colours
ruler
scissors

Teaching support

Page 1

Let's Investigate

- If appropriate, encourage the children to look for examples of angles inside the classroom, around the school and in the playground.
- You may wish to introduce to the children the terms 'acute angle' and 'obtuse angle'.
- Discuss with the children which type of angle is the most common. Can they suggest reasons for this?

Page 2

The Language of Maths

- Ensure the children are familiar with the difference between a turn (rotation) and a flip (reflection). Children also need to be able to describe a rotation using terms such as 'right angle', 'quarter turn', 'three-quarter turn', 'to the left', 'to the right', 'clockwise' and anticlockwise' (Inquisitive ant).
- Provide the children with a sheet of A4 paper that they can fold like the first sheet of paper in each pair, then flip or turn to discover the movement.

Let's Investigate

- Children need to have completed the 🐜 Let's Investigate activity on page 1 before starting on this activity, as they will need to use their right angle tester.
- Ensure the children understand how to divide and cut their A4 sheet of paper into seven shapes.

Page 3

At Home

- Once the children have completed the investigation, ensure that there is an opportunity in class for pairs or groups of children to discuss their results.

The Language of Maths

- Discuss with the children how a turn on the wheel from A to B can also be described as:
  - a three-quarters turn anticlockwise
  - a three-quarters turn to the left
  - 3 right angles anticlockwise
  - 3 right angles to the left.
- Ask the children to describe each turn on the wheel in two different ways.

Page 4

The Puzzler

- The main focus of this activity is the strategies that children develop as they play the games in order to help them win. Therefore, once pairs of children have played their four games, arrange the pairs into a group and discuss with the children the various strategies they used to help them win the game.

AfL

- Which type of angle did you find the most of? Why do you think this was?
- How has this sheet of paper been moved?
- Can you move this sheet of paper two right angles anticlockwise? How else could you describe how this sheet of paper has been moved? Is there another way to describe it?
- Describe to me the movement between these two points.
- What strategies did you use to help you win the game? Did they always work? Why not?

Answers

Page 1

Let's Investigate
Results of the investigation will vary.

Page 2

The Language of Maths

Flipped over top to bottom	Turned 1 right angle anticlockwise	Turned 2 right angles	Flipped over top to bottom	Turned 1 right angle clockwise

Let's Investigate
Results of the investigation will vary.

Page 3

At Home
Routes will vary. However, the number of turns will be the same in the morning and the afternoon.
The afternoon journey has the same number of right turns as the morning journey has left turns, and vice versa.

The Language of Maths

From A to C: $\frac{1}{2}$ turn clockwise   From B to C: $\frac{1}{4}$ turn clockwise

From A to D: $\frac{1}{4}$ turn anticlockwise   From D to A: $\frac{1}{4}$ turn clockwise

From C to D: $\frac{1}{4}$ turn clockwise   From C to A: $\frac{1}{2}$ turn clockwise

From D to B: $\frac{1}{2}$ turn clockwise   From B to D: $\frac{1}{2}$ turn clockwise

From B to A: $\frac{1}{4}$ turn anticlockwise   From D to C: $\frac{1}{4}$ turn anticlockwise

From C to B: $\frac{1}{4}$ turn anticlockwise

Other descriptions are possible.

Page 4

The Puzzler
Strategies will vary.

Inquisitive ant

anticlockwise
In the opposite direction to the one that the hands of an analogue clock move.

Prerequisites for learning

- Visualise common 2-D shapes and 3-D shapes
- Identify shapes from pictures of them in different positions and orientations
- Sort, make and describe shapes, referring to their properties
- Visualise and use everyday language to describe position, direction and movement

Resources

pencil and paper

Resource sheet 2: My notes (optional)

Resource sheet 3: Pupil self assessment booklet (optional)

Resource sheet 17: Sides and corners

ruler

circle geometric shape

camera (optional)

three paper squares, preferably each a different colour

scissors

Teaching support

Page 1

The Puzzler

- Ask the children to say how many cubes they can see.

Let's Investigate

- Provide the children with a circle geometric shape so that they can quickly and easily draw circles on which to show their patterns.

- Some children may need assistance in making a simple drawing of the hubcaps.

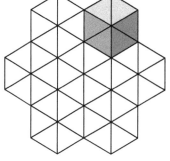

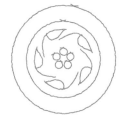

- If appropriate, the children (or an adult) can take photographs of the hubcaps using the school camera. Children can then make their drawings from these photos. Children can also make a display of both the photos and their corresponding drawings.

Page 2

Construct

- If appropriate, allow the children to work in pairs or groups to make their own origami box.
- Children can investigate other origami shapes.

Page 3

Looking for Patterns

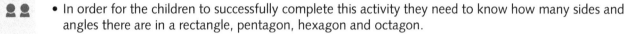

- Ensure the children can identify the position of a shape after a turn (rotation) or a flip (reflection).
- Ask the children to write a description of what each machine does to the shapes that are placed into it, i.e.
  - Machine 1: Turns 2 right angles
  - Machine 2: Reflects vertically
  - Machine 3: Turns 1 right angle to the right
  - Machine 4: Reflects each of the two parts of the whole shape horizontally.

The Language of Maths

- Ask the children to suggest how they could change the diagram so that they could spell the word 'TOTAL' the same number of times they have spelt the word 'MATHS'.

Page 4

Construct

- In order for the children to successfully complete this activity they need to know how many sides and angles there are in a rectangle, pentagon, hexagon and octagon.
- Ensure the children realise that the shapes they make are not necessarily a regular pentagon, hexagon and octagon.
- It is not possible for the children to make all four shapes using the 24 pieces on Resource sheet 17: Sides and corners – they will need to reuse some of the pieces.
- Can the children find more than one way of making each of the shapes?

At Home

- Once the children have completed the investigation, ensure that there is an opportunity in class for pairs or groups of children to discuss their results.
- Ask the children to give reasons why there are so many items in a supermarket packaged as cuboids and cylinders.

AfL

- What shapes and patterns did you see in the hubcaps on the car wheels?
- What happens to these shapes when they are put through this machine? What about this machine?
- How did you make the hexagon? What did you know about the properties of a hexagon that helped you make it?
- Why do you think items in a supermarket are very often packaged into cuboids or cylinders?

Answers

Page 1

The Puzzler
There are 14 hexagons.

Let's Investigate
Results of the investigation will vary.

Page 2

Construct
No answer required.

Page 3

Looking for Patterns

The Language of Maths
There are six different ways of spelling 'MATHS'.

Page 4

Construct

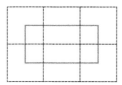 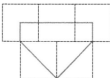

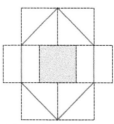 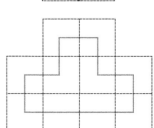

Other solutions are possible.

At Home
Results of the investigation will vary.

Inquisitive ant  rotate

To turn in a circle around a fixed point (axis) or centre.

Geometry

Prerequisites for learning

- Visualise common 2-D shapes and 3-D shapes
- Identify shapes from pictures of them in different positions and orientations
- Sort, make and describe shapes, referring to their properties
- Recognise and use whole, half and quarter turns, both clockwise and anticlockwise
- Know that a right angle represents a quarter turn
- Use the four compass directions
- Use units of time (minutes, hours, days, weeks, months) and know the relationships between them
- Tell and write the time to five minutes, including quarter past/to the hour and draw the hands on a clock face to show these times
- Compare and sequence intervals of time

Resources

pencil and paper

Resource sheet 2: My notes (optional)

Resource sheet 3: Pupil self assessment booklet (optional)

Resource sheet 18: Squares and triangles

Resource sheet 19: 1 cm squared paper

Resource sheet 20: 2 cm squared paper

Resource sheet 21: Squared dot paper

ruler

scissors

newspaper or magazine showing television listings

matchsticks

square sheet of paper

compass (optional)

computer with internet access (optional)

Teaching support

Page 1

The Language of Maths

- This activity requires children to think about the different properties of 2-D shapes and 3-D shapes such as the number of sides / faces and corners (vertices) and the types of angles.
- Once the children have finished the activity arrange them into pairs or groups to discuss and compare how they sorted the shapes.
- What if a circle and a cone were added to the four shapes?

At Home

- Once the children have completed the investigation, ensure that there is an opportunity in class for pairs or groups of children to show their drawings and discuss their results.
- If appropriate, children can carry out this investigation on the internet rather than at home.

Page 2

Construct

- Some children may need assistance with drawing the shapes onto squared paper. If this is the case, using the examples of 0 and / or 1 in the issue, show the children how to do this.

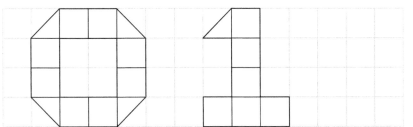

- Some of the digits can be made in more than one way. Ask the children to show these.

Let's Investigate

- In order to successfully complete this activity, children need to be able to read 12-hour digital time and identify time intervals, including those that cross the hour. If necessary, look at the television schedule with the children and work though several examples. Ensure the children realise that it is the number of complete quarter or right angle turns that they are measuring.

Page 3

The Puzzler

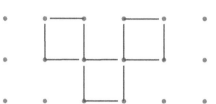

- If necessary, show the children how to draw the squares on squared dot paper.
- Ensure children realise that the solution to the last two puzzles involves squares of different sizes (a large square and a small square).

Construct

- Discuss with the children the meaning of the term 'to scale'. Although it is not expected that children will take measurements to use for drawing their plans, children should consider the relative size of the different sections and features in the school playground and show these accordingly in their plans.
- You may wish to suggest to the children that they use 1 cm or 2 cm squared paper on which to draw their plans.

Page 4

Sports Update

- There are two aspects to this activity. The first is to identify the different shapes contained in a climbing frame. The second is for the children to design their own climbing frame using as many different shapes as they can.
- Ensure that the children realise when designing their climbing frame that although they should try and include as many different shapes as possible, it still must be a climbing frame that is practical and that can be realistically used and enjoyed by children.
- You may wish to suggest to the children that they use 1 cm or 2 cm squared paper on which to draw their designs.

Let's Investigate

- If available, show the children a compass and explain to them how it works.
- Introduce the children to the four intermediate or ordinal directions, i.e. north-east (NE), north-west (NW), south-west (SW), and south-east (SE), and ask them to name things in the classroom (or outside) that they can see in each of these directions.

- Why did you sort these shapes in this way? How else could you have sorted them?
- What are the different shapes that are used for road signs? Is one shape more common than any other? Why do you think this is?
- How did you make the digit 4? What about 1? Could you have made that digit a different way? How?
- Through how many right angles did the minute hand of the clock turn during …? What other programme was the same as this?
- What was the first thing you did when you started to draw your plan of the school?
- Why do you think these shapes are most often used in climbing frames?
- Tell me something that is north / south / east / west of the classroom. North-east means the direction between north and east. Can you tell me something that is north-east of the classroom?

Answers

Page 1

The Language of Maths
Criteria for sorting will vary.

At Home
Results of the investigation will vary, but should include examples of circles, triangles and rectangles.

Page 2

Construct

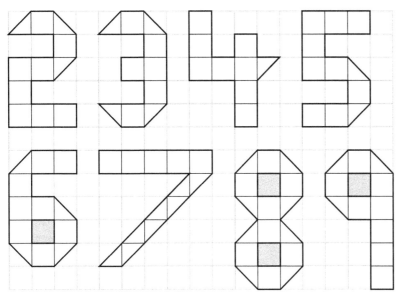

Other arrangements are possible.

Let's Investigate
Results of the investigation will vary.

Page 3

The Puzzler

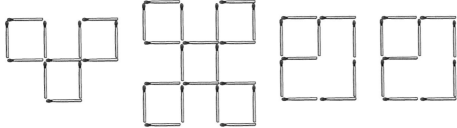

Other solutions are possible.

Construct
Plans will vary.

Page 4

Sports Update
Diagrams will vary.

Let's Investigate
Results of the investigation will vary.

Inquisitive ant  direction
The way in which someone or something moves or points.

Issue 34

Statistics

Prerequisites for learning

- Interpret and construct simple pictograms, tally charts, block diagrams and simple tables
- Ask and answer simple questions by counting the number of objects in each category and sorting the categories by quantity
- Ask and answer questions about totalling and comparing categorical data
- Solve logic puzzles

Resources

pencil and paper

Resource sheet 2: My notes (optional)

Resource sheet 3: Pupil self assessment booklet (optional)

Resource sheet 19: 1 cm squared paper (optional)

Resource sheet 20: 2 cm squared paper (optional)

ruler

toy car

apparatus to make slopes where the incline and surface can be changed

small weight to attach to toy car

counting apparatus, e.g. counters, beads, cubes

containers

computer (optional)

data handling software (optional)

Teaching support

Page 1

The Language of Maths

- If children are unfamiliar with tally charts you may wish to introduce them as a means of keeping track of the number of questions they ask each child.

Number of questions	Tally	Number
1		
2		
3		
4		

- You may wish to discuss with the children other possible questions that they might ask to try and elicit a 'yes' or 'no' response.

Focus on Science

- Children will need to undertake part of this investigation at home.
- As this activity will take a week to complete, it is recommended that it is started on a Monday.

Page 2

Around the World

- Ensure children are familiar with the five steps to the data handling cycle.
- Once the children have collected, processed, represented and interpreted the data, ask them to compare the number of bags of crisps that the average child at their school eats, with the number the average American or someone from Detroit eats.

- If appropriate, allow the children to represent their data using ICT.

The Arts Roundup

- Children need to be familiar with logic puzzles and how to use the diagram to work out the solution.

- We know the following:
  - Leo doesn't have any brothers and sisters.
  - The piano player's brothers and sisters also all learn the piano.
    Therefore, we know that Leo does not play the piano.

- We know the following:
  - The child who plays the flute is the youngest.
  - Kevin is older than the piano player.
    Therefore, we know that Kevin does not play the flute or the piano.
    So Kevin must play the violin.
    So Sam must play the piano.
    This only leaves Leo to play the flute.

	piano	flute	violin
Leo	✗		
Kevin			
Sam			

	piano	flute	violin
Leo	✗	✔	
Kevin	✗	✗	✔
Sam	✔		

Page 3

Focus on Science

- Discuss this activity with the children before they begin working independently in designing and carrying out their experiment.

- Children will need to have access to resources that will enable them to alter the incline and surface of the slope and the weight of the toy car.

Let's Investigate

- Discuss this activity with the children before they begin working independently in designing and carrying out their experiment. You may wish to suggest that they use some type of uniform counting apparatus, such as counters, beads or cubes to carry out their experiment.

Page 4

The Language of Maths

- As this activity relies heavily on children's writing skills, you may wish some children to do this activity in pairs or to complete this activity verbally rather than in writing.

- You may also want to remind the children that accurate spelling is not a priority in this activity. What is more important is being able to interpret the graph and ask suitable questions.

- If appropriate, allow the children to write their questions using ICT.

At Home

- Once the children have completed the activity, ensure that there is an opportunity in class for pairs or groups of children to discuss their results.

- Children draw a bar chart of their results.

AfL

- What did you do to get these results?
- Tell me what you found out.
- What does this mean?
- Why did you choose to record your results in this way?
- Tell me what you did for each of these steps. Why did you decide to do that?
- Tell me how you worked out the solution to this puzzle.
- What might one of the questions have been? Could it have been a different question? Why not?
- Can you tell me another time when it might be useful to record things in a tally chart?

Answers

Page 1

The Language of Maths
Results of the investigation will vary.

Focus on Science
Results of the investigation will vary.

Page 2

Around the World
Results of the investigation will vary.

The Arts Roundup

	piano	flute	violin
Leo	✗	✔	✗
Kevin	✗	✗	✔
Sam	✔	✗	✗

Page 3

Focus on Science
Results of the investigation will vary.

Let's Investigate
Results of the investigation will vary. However, generally the statement is true.

Page 4

The Language of Maths
Questions will vary, but will probably be similar to the following:
a. How many children's favourite pet is a cat?
b. How many more children prefer cats to rabbits / dogs to cats as pets?
c. How many children's favourite pet was either a bird or a cat?
d. How many children were asked about their favourite pet?

At Home
Results of the investigation will vary.

Inquisitive ant

tally
A mark or set of marks used to keep count of an amount and to represent a number. Often displayed as a set of four short vertical lines crossed by a diagonal fifth line to represent five, i.e. ⅏

Statistics

Prerequisites for learning

- Interpret and construct simple pictograms, tally charts, block diagrams and simple tables
- Ask and answer simple questions by counting the number of objects in each category and sorting the categories by quantity
- Ask and answer questions about totalling and comparing categorical data

Resources

pencil and paper

Resource sheet 2: My notes (optional)

Resource sheet 3: Pupil self assessment booklet (optional)

Resource sheet 19: 1 cm squared paper

Resource sheet 20: 2 cm squared paper

ruler

selection of travel brochures and magazines

large sheet of paper

material for making a poster

scissors

glue

white pages telephone directory

computer (optional)

data handling software (optional)

Teaching support

Page 1

Technology Today

- The most important aspect of this activity is the different ways the children record their data and sort it. Encourage the children to sort their data in as many different ways as they can think of. Examples may include:
  - usage: entertainment, cooking, cleaning, ...
  - location: kitchen, sitting room, classroom, ...

Around the World

- The purpose of this activity is for children to realise that handling data is not just about tables, graphs and charts – it is also about organising and presenting information in a clear and precise manner.
- Children can create part of their poster using ICT.

Page 2

Sports Update

- Before children set to work on this activity discuss the illustration with them. Ask: *Is it likely that someone would be able to hop more than 250 times? How many times do you think that most of your friends would be able to hop before they have to put their other foot back on the ground or they fall over?*
- Some children may need assistance with labelling the axes, particularly the vertical axis. If appropriate, discuss with the children how they may need to label the vertical axis in intervals other than 1.
- If appropriate, allow the children to display their results using ICT.

At Home

- Once the children have completed the activity, ensure that there is an opportunity in class for pairs or groups of children to discuss their results.
- If it is considered more appropriate, the children can carry out this investigation at school over the course of one or two days.

Page 3

The Arts Roundup

- Ensure children are familiar with the five steps to the data handling cycle.
- Before asking the children to repeat the investigation for the children in Year 6 or a group of adults, ask them to make a prediction.
- Discuss with the children how best to undertake the investigation for the children in Year 6 and the group of adults.

- If appropriate, allow the children to display their results using ICT.

Technology Today

- Children can be as thorough in this investigation as is appropriate. You may wish the children to find out the results by surveying the entire population of the school. Alternatively, you may wish the children to simply undertake a sample. Whichever method is decided upon, it is recommended that you discuss both these options with the children before coming to a decision.

- If appropriate, allow the children to display their results using ICT.

Page 4

Let's Investigate

- Before the children begin to work independently on this activity, ensure that they fully understand the activity.
- Once the children have answered the first two questions, encourage them to spend time on finding out other pieces of information about the names in a telephone directory.

The Language of Maths

- This activity highlights the different interpretations that different people can have of the same set of data. What is important however is that children are able to give a reasonable explanation as to what the block graph might represent, and recognise and logically explain the trends that the graph displays. Therefore, once the children have completed the activity, conduct a group discussion providing an opportunity for each child to describe their interpretation of the block graph.

AfL

- How did you sort your list? How else could you sort your list?
- Tell me the results of your investigation.
- What have you found out?
- Why did you choose to record your results in this way?
- Tell me what you did for each of these steps. Why did you decide to do that?
- Tell me the story of this graph.

Answers

Page 1

Technology Today
Lists will vary.

Around the World
Posters will vary.

Page 2

Sports Update
Results of the investigation will vary.

At Home
Results of the investigation will vary.

Page 3

The Arts Roundup
Results of the investigation will vary.

Technology Today
Results of the investigation will vary.

Page 4

Let's Investigate
Results of the investigation will vary.

The Language of Maths
Statements will vary.

Inquisitive ant

axes
The two lines on a graph, generally its extreme left and bottom lines, which are labelled showing the data categories and numerical values.

Issue 36

Statistics

Prerequisites for learning

- Interpret and construct simple pictograms, tally charts, block diagrams, bar charts and simple tables
- Ask and answer simple questions by counting the number of objects in each category and sorting the categories by quantity
- Ask and answer questions about totalling and comparing categorical data

Resources

pencil and paper
Resource sheet 2: My notes (optional)
Resource sheet 3: Pupil self assessment booklet (optional)
ruler

Teaching support

Page 1

Sports Update

- This activity is best undertaken in pairs or small groups, perhaps having the children carrying out the activity also being the competitors for the tournament.
- Prior to the children working independently on this activity ensure that they understand how the elimination tournament diagram works – perhaps referring to the illustration.
- You may need to discuss with the children what to do in the event that pairs of children 'tie' after playing 5 games, i.e. win, lose, win, lose and draw. Do they play a 'tie-breaker'?

Page 2

The Language of Maths

- Ensure children understand the glyph code, especially how the smile refers to height. You may need to have some discussion as to what constitutes 'short', 'medium' and 'tall'.
- Children need to have completed and understood this activity before starting on the 🐜 Construct activity that follows.

Construct

- Children need to have completed and understood the previous 🐜 The Language of Maths activity before starting on this activity.
- Ask the children to create their own glyph code to describe their home life, e.g. what type of housing they live in (i.e. house, flat), how many people live in their home, how many brothers and sisters they have, whether they have a garden, whether they have a pet, and so on.

Page 3

Let's Investigate

- Children need to have completed this activity before starting on 🐜 The Language of Maths activity that follows.
- Ensure children understand how to represent data in a graph before starting this activity.
- Given that the horizontal axis of the graph in the issue is labelled from 1 to 12, it is envisaged that there will not be more than 12 children in the class who have the same favourite subject.

The Language of Maths

- Children need to have completed the previous 🐛 Let's Investigate activity before starting on this activity.
- You may wish some children to do this activity in pairs or to complete the activity verbally rather than writing sentences.
- When the children have completed this activity, provide an opportunity for them to compare and discuss their sentences.

Page 4

At Home

- Ensure children understand how to represent data in a block graph before starting this activity.
- Once the children have completed the investigation, ensure that there is an opportunity in class for pairs or groups of children to share and discuss their block graphs.

The Arts Roundup

- This activity involves children interpreting data that is presented in a pictogram where the icon represents two.
- You may wish some children to do this activity in pairs or to complete the activity verbally rather than writing sentences. Encourage the children to take turns asking each other questions that involve interpreting the data, e.g. *Who sold more tickets, Tom or Leroy? How many more? Who sold six tickets? Who sold more tickets than Leroy?*

AfL

- Talk me through how you decided who would represent your class in the World Junior Noughts and Crosses Tournament. How does this chart show this?
- Tell me about this glyph / picture.
- Let me see if I can describe this picture correctly. Am I right?
- Tell me something about the information you have in this graph.
- Looking at this graph what do you notice?
- Tell me one of the sentences you write about the information in this graph / pictogram.
- Ask me a question about the information in the graph / pictogram.

Answers

Page 1

Sports Update
Results will vary.

Page 2

The Language of Maths
The picture is of a girl with an oval face, who is 6 years old. She is of medium height with curly black hair and she is right-handed.

Construct
Drawings will vary.

Page 3

Let's Investigate
Graphs will vary.

The Language of Maths
Statements will vary. However, they should reflect the data in the graph in the previous activity ( Let's Investigate).

Page 4

At Home
Block graphs will vary.

The Arts Roundup
Statements will vary.

Inquisitive ant

classify
To arrange a group of people or objects into classes or categories according to shared qualities or characteristics.

Stretch and Challenge 2 Record of completion

Class/Teacher: _____

			Names									
Domain(s)	Topic	Stretch and Challenge Issue										
Number: – Number and place value	Number	1										
	Number	2										
	Number	3										
	Number	4										
Number: – Addition and subtraction	Addition	5										
	Addition	6										
	Subtraction	7										
	Subtraction	8										
Number: – Multiplication and division	Multiplication	9										
	Multiplication	10										
	Division	11										
	Division	12										
Number: – Addition and subtraction – Multiplication and division	Mixed operations	13										
	Mixed operations	14										
	Mixed operations	15										
	Mixed operations	16										
	Mixed operations	17										

Domain(s)	Topic	*Stretch and Challenge Issue*	Names									
Number: – Fractions	Fractions	18										
	Fractions	19										
	Fractions	20										
Measurement	Length and height	21										
	Mass	22										
	Capacity and volume	23										
	Time	24										
	Measurement	25										
	Measurement	26										
Geometry: – Properties of shapes	2-D shapes	27										
	3-D shapes	28										
	Symmetry	29										
Geometry: – Position and direction	Position and direction	30										
	Movement and angle	31										
Geometry: – Properties of shapes – Position and direction	Geometry	32										
	Geometry	33										
Statistics	Statistics	34										
	Statistics	35										
	Statistics	36										

The Maths Herald

s&C Volume 2

Name:

Date:

I started this work on:

I finished this work on:

Inquisitive ant

S&C Volume 2

The Maths Herald

Name:

Date:

I started this work on:

I finished this work on:

This is what I learnt

I used these things to help me

I'd also like to say...

My teacher's comments

This is what I enjoyed the most

This is what I didn't enjoy

The work was:

too easy

just about right

too hard

What I could do next

2

2

3

3

1	2	3	4	5
6	7	8	9	10
11	12	13	14	15
16	17	18	19	20
21	22	23	24	25

1–100 number cards (2)

26	27	28	29	30
31	32	33	34	35
36	37	38	39	40
41	42	43	44	45
46	47	48	49	50

1–100 number cards (3)

51	52	53	54	55
56	57	58	59	60
61	62	63	64	65
66	67	68	69	70
71	72	73	74	75

1–100 number cards (4)

76	77	78	79	80
81	82	83	84	85
86	87	88	89	90
91	92	93	94	95
96	97	98	99	100

Six card puzzle

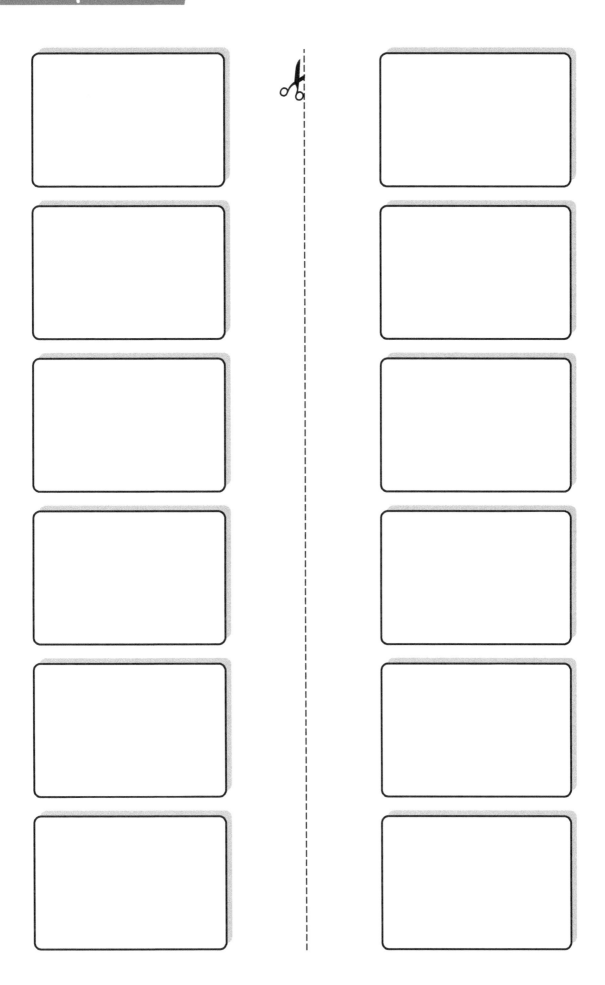

1-100 number squares

1	2	3	4	5	6	7	8	9	10
11	12	13	14	15	16	17	18	19	20
21	22	23	24	25	26	27	28	29	30
31	32	33	34	35	36	37	38	39	40
41	42	43	44	45	46	47	48	49	50
51	52	53	54	55	56	57	58	59	60
61	62	63	64	65	66	67	68	69	70
71	72	73	74	75	76	77	78	79	80
81	82	83	84	85	86	87	88	89	90
91	92	93	94	95	96	97	98	99	100

1	2	3	4	5	6	7	8	9	10
11	12	13	14	15	16	17	18	19	20
21	22	23	24	25	26	27	28	29	30
31	32	33	34	35	36	37	38	39	40
41	42	43	44	45	46	47	48	49	50
51	52	53	54	55	56	57	58	59	60
61	62	63	64	65	66	67	68	69	70
71	72	73	74	75	76	77	78	79	80
81	82	83	84	85	86	87	88	89	90
91	92	93	94	95	96	97	98	99	100

1	2	3	4	5	6	7	8	9	10
11	12	13	14	15	16	17	18	19	20
21	22	23	24	25	26	27	28	29	30
31	32	33	34	35	36	37	38	39	40
41	42	43	44	45	46	47	48	49	50
51	52	53	54	55	56	57	58	59	60
61	62	63	64	65	66	67	68	69	70
71	72	73	74	75	76	77	78	79	80
81	82	83	84	85	86	87	88	89	90
91	92	93	94	95	96	97	98	99	100

1	2	3	4	5	6	7	8	9	10
11	12	13	14	15	16	17	18	19	20
21	22	23	24	25	26	27	28	29	30
31	32	33	34	35	36	37	38	39	40
41	42	43	44	45	46	47	48	49	50
51	52	53	54	55	56	57	58	59	60
61	62	63	64	65	66	67	68	69	70
71	72	73	74	75	76	77	78	79	80
81	82	83	84	85	86	87	88	89	90
91	92	93	94	95	96	97	98	99	100

Squares

Number sentences

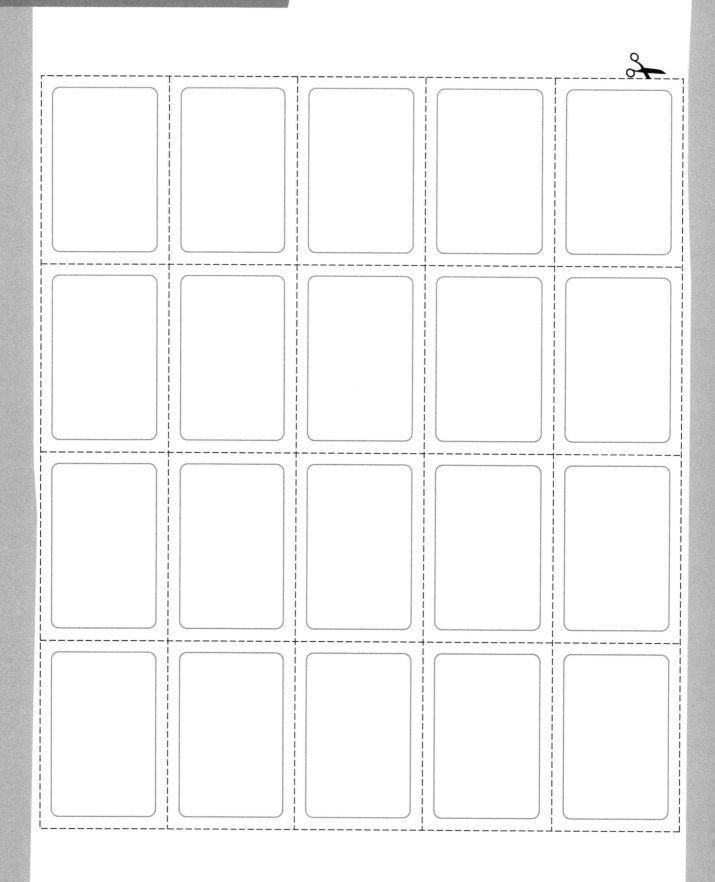

Halves and quarters

Fraction walls

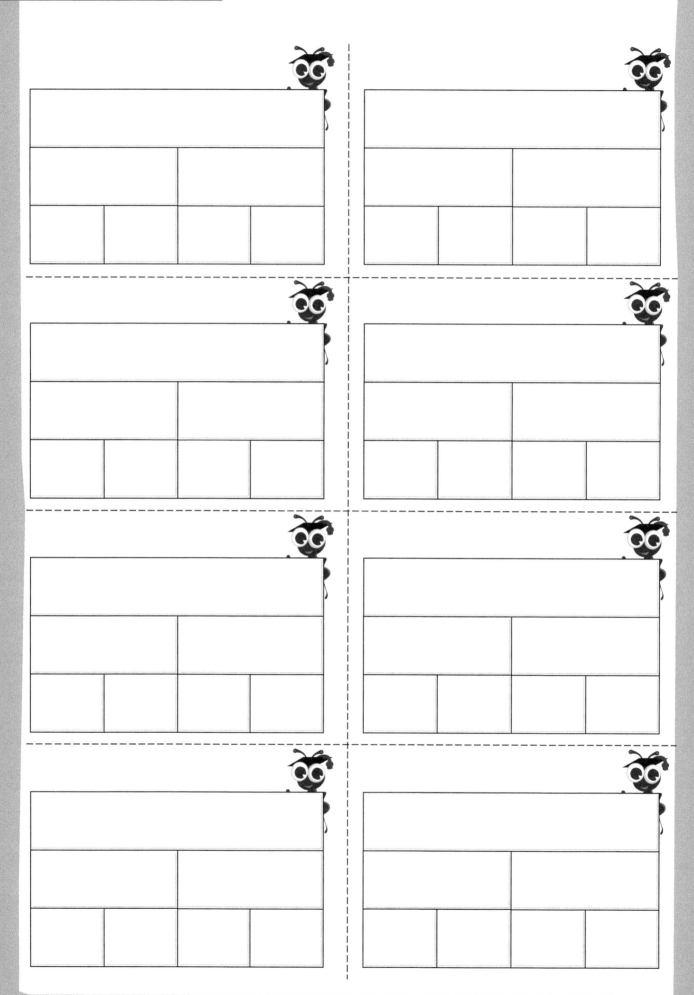

Eighths

Squares jigsaws

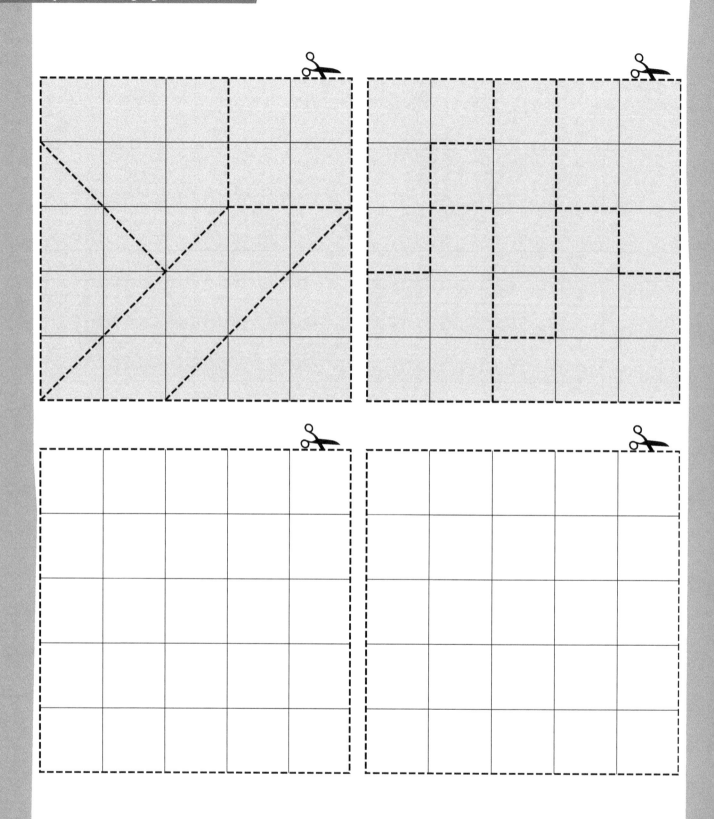

Making shapes

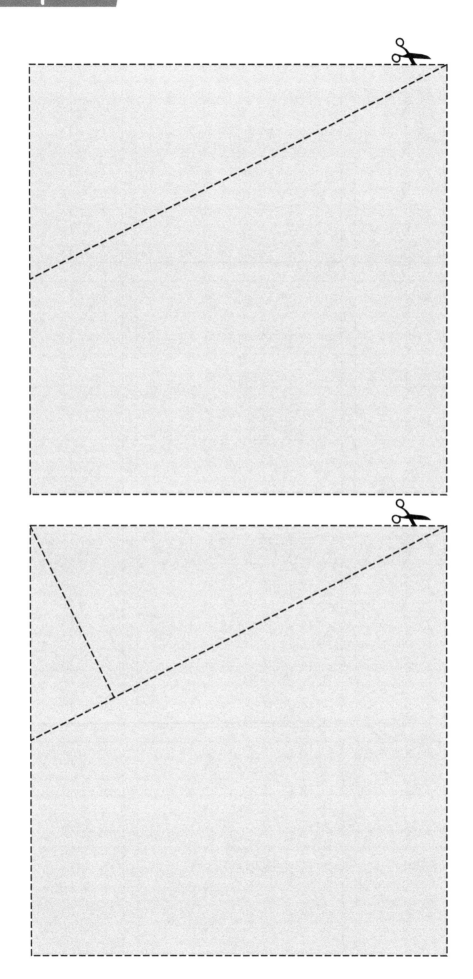

Reflective square patterns

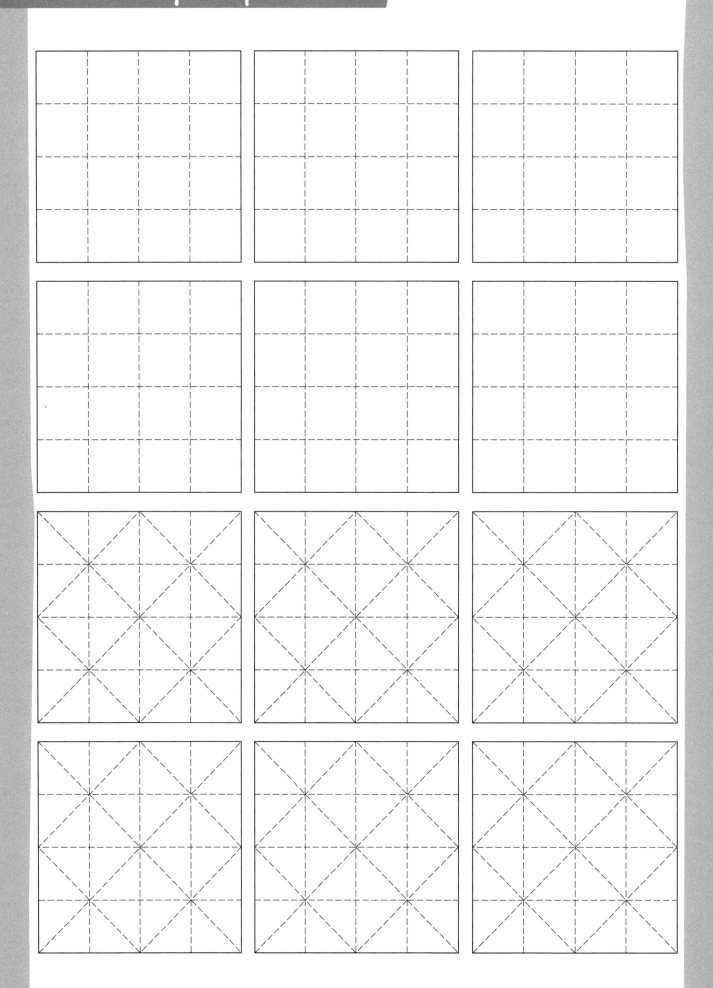

Reflective circle patterns

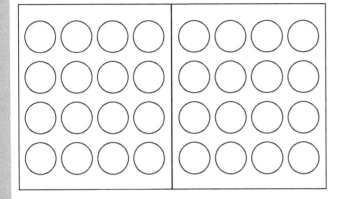
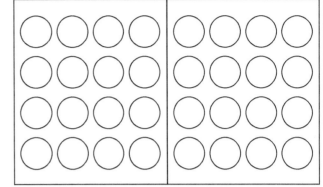

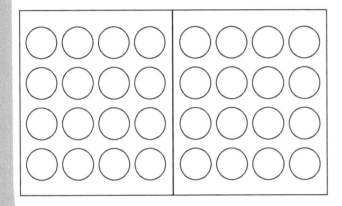
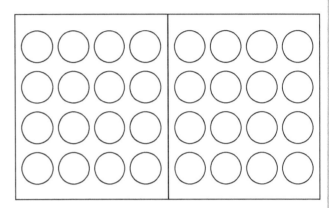

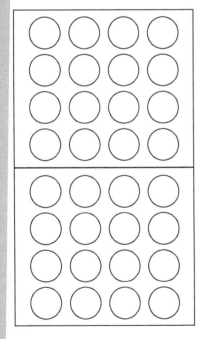
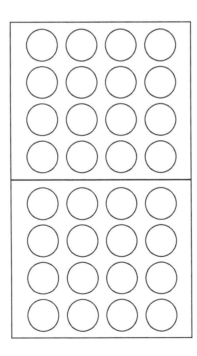
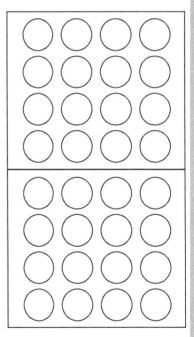

Strange grids

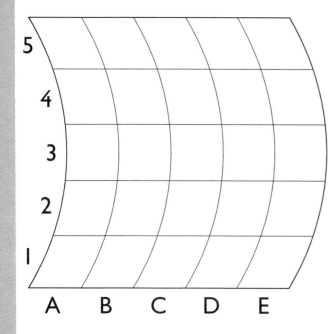

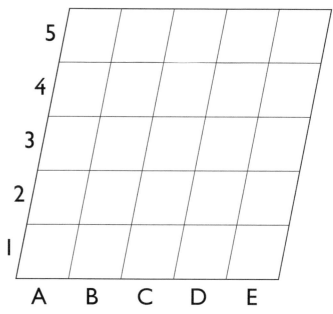

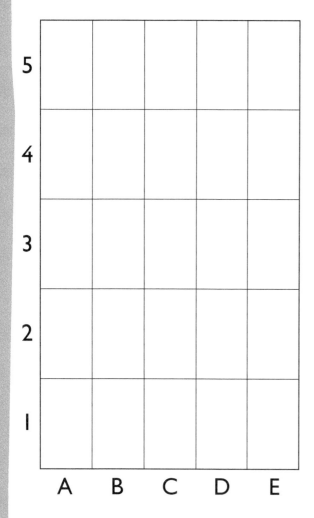

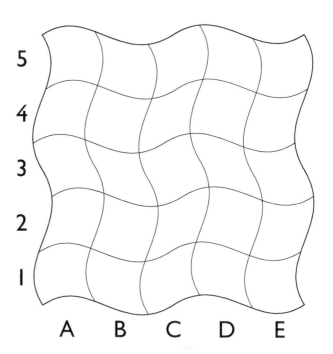

Sides and corners

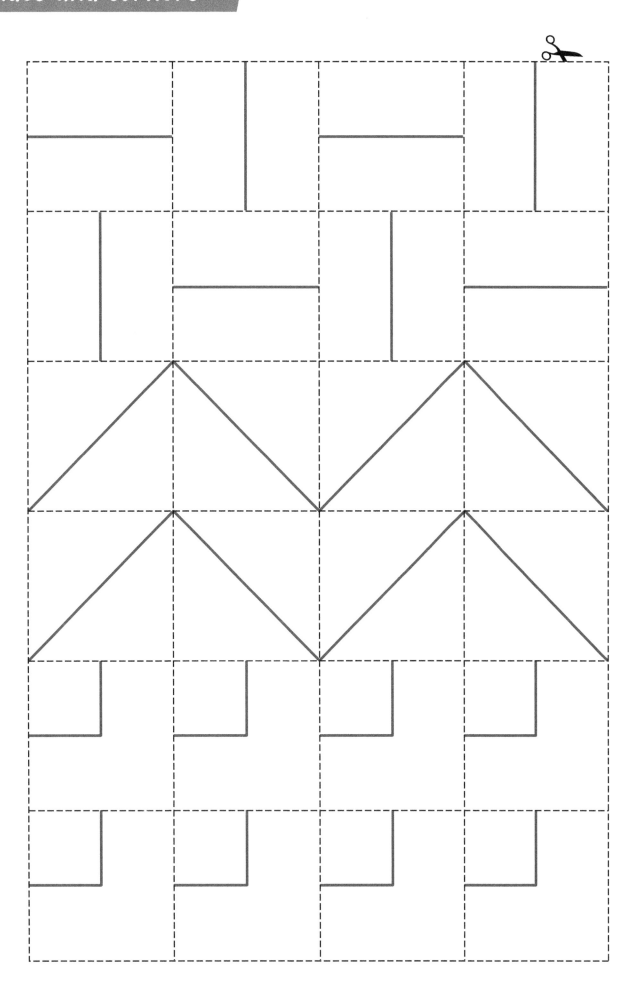

Squares and triangles

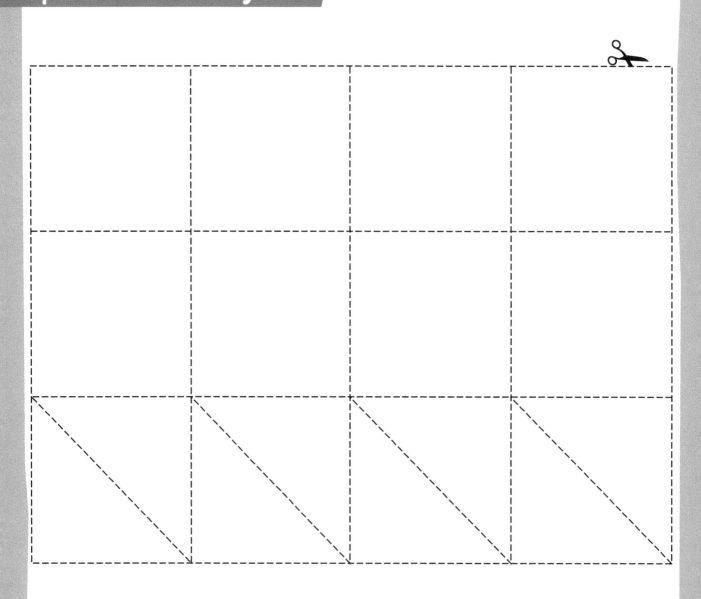

1 cm squared paper

2 cm squared paper

Squared dot paper

Triangular dot paper